THE FOUR CARDINAL MASONIC VIRTUES & THE 47th PROBLEM

Albert Pike's

"ESOTERIKA"

PART 2
THE FOUR CARDINAL MASONIC VIRTUES & THE 47th PROBLEM

ARTURO DE HOYOS, 33°, Grand Cross, K.Y.C.H.
Past Master, McAllen Lodge No. 1110, AF&AM of Texas
Grand Archivist and Grand Historian
Supreme Council, 33°, S.J., U.S.A.

Westphalia Press
Washington, D.C. • 2026

First Edition, 2026

Published in the United States of America

de Hoyos, Arturo, 1959–
Albert Pike's Esoterika: Part 2. The Four Cardinal Masonic Virtues & The 47th Problem

Title page image: "Figure des quatre Vertus" based on Jacques Patin, Ballet comique de la Royne (1582)

The poems "The 47th Problem" and "The Four Cardinal Virtues" copyright © 2025 by Arturo de Hoyos.

ISBN: 978-1-63391-968-6

Albert Pike, 33°, 1809–91
Sovereign Grand Commander, 1859–91

Photograph by Matthew B. Brady & Co., Washington, D.C
Archives of the Supreme Council, 33°, Southern Jurisdiction, USA

The 47th Problem

Within the temple of the mind
Pythagoras sought till he did find;
A noble truth was tested sound,
both rich in purpose and profound.

Where numbers danced a sacred rite,
a problem solved was brought to light,
which serves us still and brings to view
this key to numbers tried and true.

Three sides of truth, in harmony found,
a triple mystery, unveiled and crowned.
An angle's square it does unfold,
this ancient knowledge, born of old.

By the master's hand, this rule was made,
of wisdom's birth, that ne'er will fade.
From base to height, the journey's long,
whose sides reveal what makes it strong.

A path to a square, from the corners does rise,
to the center of balance, the answer lies.
A Mason's search is no less true,
for the Letter G will guide us through.

So let us take measure, and calculate,
the sides of this wonder we emulate.
With tools of virtue and mind's clear sight,
our 47th Problem will lead us right.

A lesson of balance, of mind and of heart,
a symbol of wisdom, which sets us apart,
as we travel our journey, our steps aligned,
with our triangle of truth, we seek and we find.

The Four Cardinal Virtues

In the quiet depths, where virtues rise,
four pillars stand beneath the skies.
Each one a guide, each one a key,
to navigate life, and make men free.

*T*EMPERANCE *whispers, soft and clear,*
"balance in all," to hold what's dear.
Not in excess, nor to deny,
but view the world with a moderate eye.

*F*ORTITUDE, *steadfast as the mountain stone,*
gives strength to carry, though alone,
through storm and struggle, fear and pain,
with courage to rise again, again.

*P*RUDENCE *walks with a thoughtful grace,*
weighing each step, in time and place.
She knows the cost of every choice,
and listens well to Wisdom's voice.

*J*USTICE, *with scales in steady hand,*
weighs every deed, both small and grand.
She seeks the truth, no mask, no guise,
her voice is strong and speaks no lies.

Together they stand, Temperance and Fortitude,
Prudence and Justice, in their noble mood,
with lanterns ablaze during the darkest night,
to guide us ever with steadfast light.

That men of intelligence see nothing of value as the subject of study and reflection in the symbols of the Blue Lodge ought not to seem strange to anyone who reads the monitorial explanations. [Thomas Smith] Webb, to whom Masonry is indebted(?) for the most of them, was profoundly ignorant of the ancient symbolism; of no reading in the Classics, knowing nothing in regard to the old philosophers and the old religions. In permitting him to explain her symbols, Masonry was as unfortunate as she has been in permitting her jurisprudence to find for commentators only men of no knowledge of the principles either of the English or Roman law: and those who have undertaken to write upon the subject of Masonic symbolism have either kept within the circle, traced by Webb, or indulged in the fantastic vagaries of astronomical interpretations, or in excursions into the boundless realms of fancy and imagination, or have involved themselves in an incomprehensible network of mathematical figures, a maze of circles, triangles, and other figures that no sane human intellect can find a meaning in, in part intended to elucidate the 47th problem of Euclid by an obtuse-angled triangle.

—Albert Pike, *The Symbolism of the Blue Degrees of Freemasonry* (1888)

When the Freemasons shall have faith in their creed and mission, and men of faith to lead them, Masonry will be what it has the right to be, and what, we do believe, God means it to be, a mighty and beneficent power in every civilized land; its Holy Empire everywhere, the empire of intellect, reason, philosophy, of wise morality, and pure religion.

—Albert Pike, ritual of the 32°, Master of the Royal Secret (1879)

CONTENTS

PREFACE

In 1887, aware that his life was nearing its end, Albert Pike undertook what he regarded as one of his most significant intellectual endeavors: the composition of a manuscript entitled *Esoterika: The Symbolism of the Blue Degrees of Freemasonry*. This work would come to represent his most comprehensive and critical examination of the symbolic and philosophical underpinnings of Craft, or Blue Lodge, Masonry, the foundational three degrees upon which all of Freemasonry is built.

In the manuscript's introduction, Pike recounted the long trajectory of his Masonic studies, which had spanned decades of research, reflection, and critical engagement. Initially, he approached the Fraternity's teachings with difference, accepting many interpretations disseminated by prominent Masonic lecturers—whom he sardonically referred to as the "sir oracles" of the Craft. However, as his intellectual vigor deepened, Pike began to question and eventually reject these conventional views, many of which were rooted less in historical or philosophical substance than in uncritical tradition, speculative fancy, or outright invention.

Pike lamented that the symbols and allegories embedded in the ritual *monitors* (guide books) of his time had been subjected only to superficial and often banal interpretations. These were, in his estimation, repeated by rote and accepted uncritically by the majority of initiates, who showed little interest in probing the more profound meanings veiled within the rituals. The resulting atmosphere of intellectual complacency and symbolic trivialization deeply troubled Pike. His dissatisfaction with these shallow expositions drove him to pursue a deeper and systematic exploration of Masonic symbolism— one that sought to recover what he believed were genuine esoteric truths long obscured by centuries of misinterpretation. For Pike, the true value of Masonic symbols was not in their outward repetition, but in the hidden moral, philosophical and spiritual insights they preserved—insights that had become increasingly opaque even to those charged with their safeguarding.

He was uniquely positioned to benefit from the emergence of modern Masonic historiography, which was undergoing significant development at precisely the time he embarked upon his own investigations into the origins and meanings of Masonic symbolism. This fortuitous historical alignment enabled him not only to draw from the growing body of critical and academic work on Freemasonry but also to contribute meaningfully to that discourse through his own original research and interpretations.

With a deep sense of purpose, he undertook a systematic exploration of the earliest known rituals, emblems, and symbolic constructs associated with the Craft. Rather than viewing these artifacts as isolated relics, he attempted to consider them within the broader intellectual, philosophical, and cultural contexts from which they had emerged. This contextual approach allowed him to discern what he perceived to be a deliberate and intrinsic relationship between the symbols employed within the Masonic tradition and the abstract principles or truths they were intended to signify. This was a purposeful integration of form and meaning, reflective of the philosophy underlying the Craft. As his investigations progressed, he began to share his findings through a series of lectures given in his capacity as Provincial Grand Master of the Royal Order of Scotland. His presentations aimed to uncover the genuine historical origins and offered reasoned, systematic interpretations of the Craft's foundational symbols—many of which he believed had been obscured through layers of allegory and time.

Pike considered this knowledge as genuinely esoteric in nature—truths accessible only through disciplined inquiry, philosophical reasoning, and personal preparation. Although he had travelled extensively throughout the States and delivered numerous lectures on the symbolic and philosophical dimensions of Freemasonry, he never committed a comprehensive and systematic exposition of his ideas to a single unified text. Despite the breadth of his spoken contributions, his insights remained dispersed across various lectures, personal notes, and oral traditions. Well-versed in the allegory of the master architect of Solomon's Temple—whose premature death resulted in the tragic loss of a profound and sacred secret—Pike became increasingly concerned that his own intellectual legacy might likewise be lost upon his death, particularly given the esoteric nature of his work and its reliance on oral transmission. Motivated by this concern he compiled a rough manuscript to preserve the core of his symbolic and philosophical discoveries. This was then transcribed by the Supreme Council's calligrapher, Ill. Edwin B. Mac Grotty, 33°, who also enriched it with hand-drawn illustrations. Upon completion the rough manuscript was destroyed. Mac Grotty's attractively-prepared text was beautifully bound in blue leather in 1888, and remains in the Archives of the House of the Temple.

To frame his work he chose the title *Esoterika*, a term which not only signaled the subject matter, but also cleverly included a hidden linguistic element: the deliberate spelling with a "k" allowed for the formation of an anagram—"seek ratio"—which served as a subtle exhortation to his readers to pursue reason and rationality in their interpretive efforts. In this way he aligned himself with the Enlightenment ideals of logic and inquiry, positioning his scholarship as both a continuation of and a contribution to the intellectual heritage of Freemasonry. A second manuscript copy was sent to London, where it was studied by Pike's friend, the prominent barrister Robert Freke Gould, who was also the foremost English Masonic historian. It was also studied by George William Speth, secretary of Quatuor Coronati Lodge 2076, the world's premiere Masonic lodge. Both men, renowned for their rigorous standards and discerning judgment, were profoundly impressed by the intellectual depth and interpretive sophistication of Pike's work. They described Pike's work as an incomparable work of scholarship. Gould unapologetically gushed, "There is no one among our British Masonic writers who could have written up to the level of your performance," while Speth admitted that it "stands as pre-eminent as the most philosophic and admirable work of the kind I have every perused."[1]

I first learned of *Esoterika* in 1988 (a century after the manuscript was completed), when I saw its entry in Ray Baker Harris' *Bibliography of the Writings of Albert Pike* (1957), but it wasn't until 1993 that I had an opportunity to read it. In that year I travelled from my home in McAllen, Texas, to Washington D.C. to attend "Masonic Week" (an annual gathering of sundry organizations) and arranged to speak with Reynold J. "Dick" Matthews, 33°, the Scottish Rite's Grand Archivist. At the time my research was focused on the formidable task of "reverse-engineering" Pike's *Morals and Dogma*—that is, tracing the intellectual and textual sources used in its creation, with the hope of producing and annotated edition.[2] My periodic visits to Washington, D.C. afforded invaluable access to his personal library and manuscript collection, offering a glimpse into some of the sources that underpinned his philosophy. Brother Matthews, with whom I shared a mutual interest in the German language, allowed me to study the manuscript of *Esoterika*

---

[1] Arturo de Hoyos, *Albert Pike's Esoterika: The Symbolism of the Blue Degrees of Freemasonry* (Washington, D.C.: Scottish Rite Research Society, 2005), xxxvi, xxxvii

[2] Published as Arturo de Hoyos, *Albert Pike's Morals and Dogma: Annotated Edition* (Washington, D.C.: Supreme Council. 33°, S.J., 2011)

in full, on the condition that I did so seated beside his office desk. The following day—perhaps wearied by audible injections at "aha!" moments—Matthews suggested, with a mix of patience and amusement, that I continue my reading in the Library. That visit marked the beginning of my relationship with *Esoterika*, a work that had been long overshadowed by *Morals and Dogma*, although it is equally, if not more so, valuable.

Pike was firmly against the wide distribution of *Esoterika*. He forbade the "multiplication of copies of the book, or any part of it by printing" and even restricted distribution in part by manuscript by anyone who was not "fit and qualified to teach and instruct his Brethren." This restriction created something of a dilemma. I was forcibly struck by the manuscript's importance and richness, as I realized that it could help provide further light and knowledge. During Pike's lifetime the Scottish Rite was a modest institution comprising only a few thousand members. But by the 20th century the Rite had grown dramatically, claiming hundreds of thousands of members. The practical result of a continued restriction meant that the overwhelming majority Scottish Rite Masons would remain permanently excluded from the insights contained in *Esoterika*. In effect, the manuscript risked becoming a relic—highly significant yet inaccessible. Pike considered it his personal intellectual property, and even went so far as to pronounce a curse upon anyone who would disseminate the text against his wishes. If his language was rhetorical it still underscores the gravity with which Pike viewed the sanctity of the work.

As sometimes happens in life, however, the universe provided a solution. A confluence of circumstances, both institutional and personal, began to shift the destiny of the text's future. In 1999 I was honored to accept the position of Grand Archivist and Grand Historian of the Supreme Council, 33°, Southern Jurisdiction, a role that placed me at the very heart of the institutional and intellectual legacy of Albert Pike. I soon initiated a discussion with Grand Commander C. Fred Kleinknecht, 33°, concerning the potential publication of *Esoterika*. In our conversation I made two critical observations that influenced our deliberation. First, I pointed out that substantial portions of *Esoterika* had already appeared—albeit in altered form—in Pike's various lectures delivered to the Royal Order of Scotland. Second, I noted that select elements of his research had been integrated into his revisions of the Scottish Rite rituals themselves. Thus, although the complete corpus of Pike's ideas was only preserved in the text of *Esoterika*, its core ideas were diffused into Pike's wider body of Masonic work.

Grand Commander Kleinknecht was supportive of the idea and encouraged me to prepare the manuscript for publication. He kindly offered to either have the Supreme Council print my completed work, or to help me find another publisher. Unfortunately, other projects, the demands of work, and a busy home life delayed publication. During that time I completed reading all of Pike's extant Masonic manuscripts—a task that further deepened my understanding of his philosophy.

Upon Grand Commander Kleinknecht's retirement in 2003 I returned to the idea with focused energy. In a discussion with his successor, Grand Commander Ronald A. Seale, 33°, I revisited the issue of publication. We weighed the potential benefits and drawbacks of printing the manuscript, when I suggested that the work could be printed under the auspices of the Scottish Rite Research Society, a venue that would ensure that Pike's work would be presented as a serious contribution to Masonic thought.

The timing was fortuitous. By the early 21st century, a fresh spirit of inquiry and openness had begun to infuse the grand bodies of Freemasonry in the United States. Masonic research—long constrained by a tradition of institutional caution—was undergoing a renaissance, with more material published about the Fraternity in the preceding decade than in the previous half-century. Grand Commander Seale agreed with my proposal, and I completed the work.

Thus, in 2005, the first-ever authorized edition of *Esoterika* was published. To my great satisfaction—and, I believe, to the benefit of the Craft in general—the book quickly emerged as one of Pike's most popular and widely studied writings. So influential did it become that it serves as the cornerstone of the Supreme Council's *Master Craftsman Education Program*. Far from diminishing Pike's legacy, its publication enhanced it, revealing deeper dimensions of his philosophical vision to generations of Masonic students. In retrospect, I can only hope that I met the standard Pike set for those he considered "fit and qualified" to interpret and disseminate his teachings. And I confess, with both humility and a touch of humor, that I have silently prayed that Pike might revoke—or at least suspend—the "curse" he placed upon me for publishing the book against his will.

After completing *Esoterika* Pike lived only three more years. For over a century, it appeared that his work in esoteric research had concluded with that volume. The "book," so to speak, seemed closed.

However, I encountered compelling evidence to the contrary—evidence to suggest that Pike had, in fact, continued his inquiries beyond *Esoterika*, though his further studies were unknown to scholars and archivists alike. The discovery came through my very dear and late friend, Kent Logan Walgren (1947–2003), a retired attorney and judge from Salt Lake City. Kent was not only a devoted student of Masonic literature but also the proprietor of two antiquarian bookshops. Over the course of more than two decades of friendship, we had exchanged many Masonic texts—some though purchase, others by trade, and still others offered to me as thoughtful gifts. After returning from a trip Kent contacted me about an unusual and previously unattributed bound manuscript he had acquired. The title, *The Four Cardinal Virtues and the 47th Problem*, was unfamiliar to both of us. Kent noted that the handwriting was small and difficult to decipher—but he believed the text was a treatise on what he called "moral Masonry."

Upon acquiring the volume, I immediately recognized something extraordinary. The binding was identical to that of *Esoterika*, and more significantly, the handwriting was unmistakably that of Albert Pike. Concerned that the manuscript might have once have belonged to the Supreme Council and become separated from its archives, I conducted an exhaustive review of the three printed bibliographies of Pike's books and manuscripts.[3] To my astonishment and relief, there was no reference to the manuscript whatsoever. There is no indication within the text itself as to its provenance, ownership history, or intended recipient. The absence of any institutional markings or archival records suggested that the manuscript had never been a part of the official collections of the Supreme Council. Had it been prepared as a private text which Pike presented or loaned to someone? Always confidential about his sources, Kent declined to reveal the name or location of the previous owner. But he did tell me that the person from whom it was purchased said it belonged to a deceased relative who was a Scottish Rite Mason during Pike's lifetime.

Unfortunately, this is all I know about the origins of the book you are now reading. For years I considered keeping this treasure private, but I've realized that doing so would be no different than Pike keeping

---

[3] *Libraries of the Supreme Council for the 33d Degree for the Southern Jurisdiction of the United States at Washington. First Division. The Pike Library of the Supreme Council* (New York: J.J. Little, 1884); William R. Boyden, *Bibliography of the Writings of Albert Pike. Poetry, Music, Manuscripts* (Washington, D.C.: The Supreme Council, 33°, 1921); Ray Baker Harris, ed., *Bibliography of the Writings of Albert Pike. Centennial Edition* (Washington, D.C.: The Supreme Council, 33°, 1957)

the first part of *Esoterika* private. By fortune, or synchronicity, I am thus able to share all of *Esoterika*, and offer this second treasure to the Masonic world, commending its readers to "seek reason" as they study the rich moral philosophy of the Craft.

As with several of my other works, my footnotes reveal the sources of Pike's quotations, as well as offer further information for reference and study. In editing his text, I have corrected, modernized and expanded his references, using pipes to indicate my own editorial insertions, e.g., |phronēsis|, whereas Pike used brackets, i.e., [].

INTRODUCTION

Three years before his death, and after serving nearly thirty years as Sovereign Grand Commander of the Scottish Rite, Albert Pike compiled a study which he called *Esoterika: The Symbolism of the Blue Degrees of Freemasonry* (1888). This work, which he never intended to publish, preserved his private reflections and insights in various topics, including "The Compasses and the Square," "The Weapons and Blows of the Assassins," "The Three Grips," "The Substitute for the Master's Word," and more. Pike's analysis delved beyond what had been done in the past, and provided valuable insights and fresh perspectives. As a part of his approach he looked into the earliest known Masonic appearances of the subjects and considered them in light of contemporary sources. His discoveries led him to believe that although Freemasonry preserved ancient symbolism the deeper meanings of many symbols had been forgotten or lost. Although he believed he had rediscovered the true meanings behind some symbols, he also confessed that other enigmas remained.

The Four Cardinal Virtues

Among the subjects which begged for a fuller investigation is the deeper significance of the "Four Cardinal Virtues" (temperance, fortitude, prudence, and justice), central concepts in classical philosophy which also stand as enduring pillars within the ethical framework of Freemasonry. These virtues, which have a lineage founded in the bedrock of Western moral philosophy, may be briefly described as follows: Temperance is the virtue of self-control, moderation, and balance. It concerns exercising restraint, especially in regard to desires and pleasures. It encourages one to avoid excess and to make choices that promote long-term well-being over short-term gratification. Fortitude refers to the strength of character to endure difficulties, challenges, and adversity. It enables a person to stand firm in the face of fear, pain, or hardship, and to continue striving toward good even when the path is difficult. Prudence is the exercise of practical wisdom or the ability to make good decisions. It concerns knowing what is right and acting accordingly, especially when faced with difficult situations. Finally, Justice is giving each person what is properly due. It is the virtue of fairness, treating others with equality, and respecting their rights.

Mentioned in the Entered Apprentice degree, in most American grand lodges, these virtues are connected to four "points of entrance," or "points of initiation," denominated guttural, pectoral, manual and pedal (corresponding to the throat, breast, hands and feet). Allowing that the latter have ritual significance, Pike further believed that the virtues themselves were of the utmost importance.

First known collectively from Plato's *Republic* (Book 4:426–35), which was composed around 375 BC, the virtues may be even older. The *Republic* introduced them as political virtues necessary in a theoretical ideal state, where they were enumerated and contrasted: wisdom (prudence) is necessarily applied to the rulers and deals in reason; courage (fortitude), to the military and the spirited part of the soul; discipline (temperance) is reflected in the universal equilibrium which allows the state to function harmoniously; and finally, justice is the harmonious balance of all faculties, and requires citizens of all classes to attend to the performance of their duties for the good of all.

Plato's student, Aristotle, further refined these virtues in his *Nicomachean Ethics* (ca. 350 BC), emphasizing the role of habituation and rational deliberation in their development. The virtues were not seen as mere ideals to admire but as capacities to be cultivated through practice and moral effort. This Hellenic inheritance was passed on to Roman thinkers, most notably Cicero, who in *De Officiis* (44 BC) emphasized the cardinal virtues as the bedrock of civic duty and personal integrity. Cicero's Latin framing of these virtues—*prudentia, temperantia, fortitudo,* and *iustitia*—would prove deeply influential on medieval and Renaissance thought. Recognized and acknowledged by the Stoics and other philosophers by the first century, BC, they were introduced to the Jewish Apocrypha, where they were ostensibly presented by the wise King Solomon: "And if a man love righteousness her labours are virtues: for she teacheth temperance and prudence, justice and fortitude: which are such things, as men can have nothing more profitable in their life" (Wisdom of Solomon 8:7). Adopted by early Christians, St. Ambrose (Bishop of Milan from 374–397), called them "cardinal virtues," when he compared them with the Beatitudes in his *Expositio evangelii secundum Lucam:*

> Now we must discover how Saint Luke manages to condense the eight Beatitudes into four. There are, as we know, four cardinal virtues: temperance, justice, prudence, fortitude. Anyone who is poor in spirit is not going to be greedy or miserly; one who weeps is not arrogant or over-bearing, but gentle and peaceable; one

who mourns, humbles himself. A person who is just does not refuse to give something that was intended to be given for the general good. One who is merciful gives freely of his own; and one who gives freely of his own property is not likely to covet the property of someone else or to lay snare for them.

All the virtues are linked together, so that in having one you may find that you have several others. The saints each have their own proper virtue; but the virtue that embraces most other, will be the most richly rewarded.[4]

St. Ambrose called them "cardinal" (from Latin, *cardo*, "a hinge") since they are hinged, or connected, one with another, as he noted, "All the virtues are linked together, so that in having one you may find that you have several others." They are thus interconnected and complementary, each reinforcing the others. Prudence helps guide justice, fortitude enables us to uphold justice, and temperance supports the other virtues by keeping our desires in check. By cultivating these virtues, individuals can live a life of moral integrity, make wise decisions, treat others with fairness, face challenges with resilience, and live in a balanced and harmonious way. Forming a backbone of ethical and virtuous living, they offer a framework for becoming the best version of oneself, which is the goal of Freemasonry.

Early Masonic Usage
The Four Cardinal Virtues serve not merely as inherited abstractions but as active working tools of the moral builder. Their appearance in Masonic lectures, tracing boards, and charges reflects their function as guides to self-governance and upright conduct. In ritual, they are not taught as rigid rules but as living principles to be internalized and exemplified. Temperance encourages the moderation of passions; Fortitude emboldens one to persevere in adversity; Prudence teaches the initiate to act with foresight and moral intelligence; and Justice commands us to render to every man his due.

It is difficult to say when the four cardinal virtues were introduced to Freemasonry. The Rev. George Oliver asserted that during the Eighteenth Century the "the symbols of the four Cardinal Virtues were

---

[4] Ide M. Ni Riain, trans., *Commentary of Saint Ambrose on the Gospel according to Saint Luke* (Dublin, Ireland: Elo Press, 2001), Bk. 5:62–63

delineated by an acute angle, variously disposed."[5] Although he didn't reveal his source, Oliver's remark alluded to four symbols, i.e., "The Free-Mason's Signs," appearing in *The Grand Mystery of Free-Masons Discover'd* (1724). The "signs" were "A Gutteral," "A Pedistal," "A Manual," and "A Pectoral."[6] If any true allusion to the virtues was intended, it is vague at best. Similarly indistinct was the *Dissertation delivered upon Masonry deliver'd to a Lodge in America* (1734)[7] which stated "I beseech you, to persevere in the Constant practice of every virtue," without naming any one in particular. In1757 we have something more concrete when Thomas Dunckerley extolled the "Practice of Piety, Temperance, Fortitude, and Justice." Omitting his explanation of the first, Dunckerley stated:

> Temperance is the second Virtue I am to take Notice of, and this more immediately concerns the Duty we owe to ourselves. It does not deny us the Use of any of those Blessings that the Almighty has in his great Goodness bestowed on us: No; it only teaches us not to enjoy them to Excess, and to do nothing that will prejudice our Reason, our Healths, our Families, or our Fortunes.
>
> Prudence is the Parent of Temperance. It is Prudence that will direct us to the Choice of our Company before our Liquor, and to shun all Occasions that may lead to Excess. It is too true, that *evil Communication corrupts good Manners*: And however singular we may appear to be in the Opinion of unthinking Men, yet it must be a secret Satisfaction to every Mason, when he considers that exact Decorum and Regularity with which our Meetings are always attended; where the strictest Temperance is observ'd; where nothing profane, immoral, or ludicrous, is permitted; nor any thing offer'd to disturb the Harmony of our Society. Let us then, my Brethren, continue to persevere in this and every other

---

[5] George Oliver, *The Revelations of a Square* (London: Richard Spencer, 1855), 17–18.

[6] *The Grand Mystery of Free-Masons Discover'd* (1724), in Douglas Knoop, G.P. Jones, and Douglas Hamer, *The Early Masonic Catechisms* 2d ed. (Manchester University Press, 1963), 77.

[7] See Shawn Eyer, "A *Dissertation Upon Masonry, 1734*, with Commentary and Notes," in *Philalethes: The Journal of Masonic Research and Letters* 68 (2015): 62–75

Virtue. But this requires Fortitude, which is the next Virtue I am to take Notice of.

True Fortitude comprehends Patience, and an unshaken Courage. There is no Condition of Life in which it is possible for a Man to be cast, but the Virtue of true Fortitude (like a true Friend) will go along with him: It will sooth his Sorrows, and alleviate his Griefs. If Death deprive him of his Friend or near Relation; if a Bed of Sickness be his Lot; if his House be rifled, or a Prison his Habitation, he remains calm and undisturb'd, nor do his Spirits rise and fall with his Condition; he relies on his Innocence and his God, and on that / Foundation stands fixed as a Rock...

The Remaining Part of my Discourse is to explain Justice in the general Sense of the Word, or the Duty we owe to Mankind. It includes all the social Virtues. But as Time will not permit me to expatiate on each particular Branch, I shall be as brief as possible. But what have I undertaken? Love presents itself, and claims my Attention. How can I attempt to desire that which the Greatest Men have in vain endeavour'd to describe? This however shall not discourage me. Tho' Language is too weak, and Words fall short, so that we cannot paint this heavenly Virtue in its true Colours, since it can only be known to those whose Hearts as susceptible of so divine an Impression; yet the principal Advantages arising from it to Society demand our Consideration at this Time....[8]

An early hint at ritual use appears in the initiatory prayer in *Three Distinct Knocks* (1760), which paraphrases 2 Peter 1:6; it mentions both temperance and prudence. An engraved English lodge certificate, dated 1766, includes a depiction of the Four Cardinal Virtues, although this is not evidence that they were mentioned in a ritual.[9] According to one author, in 1763 William Hutchinson introduced "the 'three G. Pillars' the

---

[8] "The Moral Part of Masonry Explained in a Charge Deliver'd to the Lodge of Free and Accepted Masons, Held at the Pope's-Head in Plymouth By Thomas Dunckerley, Master of the Lodge. June the 24th, 5757," reprinted in Róbert Péter and Cécile Révauger, *British Freemasonry, 1717–1813. Volume 1: Institutions* (London: Routledge, 2017), 75–80.

[9] See photo in Alexander Piatigorsky, *Who's Afraid of Freemasons?* (1997; reprint ed., Barnes & Noble, 2005), 207.

'four cardinal virtues' and gave to the star its Christian significance."[10] To the contrary, Hutchinson didn't become a Mason until 1770, although an explanation of the virtues did appear his *The Spirit of Masonry* (1775), where each is named, described, and connected to the symbol of the "Blazing Star."[11]

William Preston's *Illustrations of Masonry* (1772) toasted "the cardinal virtues" without defining them, and in the sixth edition of his *Illustrations* (1781) wrote that "the cardinal virtues do not escape our notice" although they are not further explained. Fortunately, a number of Preston's rituals survive which provide us with more concrete information. By 1787 Preston was working his "Harodim system" of Freemasonry and, to assist in teaching his lectures, he printed small *Syllabus Books* which, which included an abbreviated cipher text.[12] The following extract, from the catechism of Preston's First Degree lecture, provides an early Masonic inclusion of the Cardinal Virtues.

> Explain Temperance.
>> By this virtue we govern our passions, and check our unruly desires; the health of the body and the dignity of the mind are equally concerned in its observance.
> How is this applied in Masonry?
>> To the guttural point it applies; for vicious habits, and irregular indulgences might throw us off our guard, and, by a breach of fidelity, subject us to the penalty of the obligation; to which that point more immediately refers.
> Explain Fortitude.
>> By fortitude we are taught to resist temptation, and encounter dangers, with spirit and resolution: alike distinct from rashness and cowardice; when possessed of this virtue, we are seldom shaken, and never overthrown by the storms which surround us.
> How is this applied in Masonry?
>> To the pectoral point it alludes, for true courage can only centre in the heart, where our treasure is lodged; and from which cabinet our secrets can never be extorted, without

---

[10] Jacob Norton, "Principles, Not Forms, the True Landmarks of Masonry," in *The Masonic Eclectic: Gleanings from the Harvest Field of Masonic Literature* vol. 3 (May, 1867), No. 5, 146.

[11] William Hutchinson, *The Spirit of Masonry in Moral and Elucidatory Lectures* (London: J. Wilkie and W. Goldsmith, 1775), 112–13

[12] Colin Dyer, *William Preston and his Work* (London: Lewis Masonic, 1987) provides an excellent biography, as well as a decryption of his ritual text.

that lasting pain to the mind which the pectoral point so strongly inculcates.

Explain Prudence.

By prudence we are taught to regulate our conduct by the rules of right reason; judge and determine with propriety, in every measure, with respect to the general good: this virtue therefore constitutes the best jewel that can adorn the human frame.

How is this applied in Masonry?

To the manual point it applies; for where can prudence be more properly exercised, than when we pledge conformity to a solemn vow, with the right hand, which ought never to seal what the heart is not inclined to perform.

Explain Justice.

By this virtue we render to every man his due without distinction; it is not only consistent with divine and moral law, but is the standard and cement of civil society; without justice universal confusion would ensue; lawless force would overcome equity; and social intercourse no longer exist.

How is this applied in Masonry?

To the pedal point it applies, for when placed at the North East corner of the Lodge, resting secure on the foundation stone of the building, that virtue is warmly recommended, in the prosecution of our journey through life to secure the esteem, and merit the approbation of men.

Thus we illustrate the means which the wise founders of the art have adopted, to inculcate a lasting impression of our tenets, and enable them to maintain the character of true and faithful amongst Masons.[13]

---

[13] Dyer, *William Preston*, 204

KIBCD HELBEE, SECT VI.

CLAUSE III.

Wt impress mind

Princ pints

Name

Exp

    Wt allud

    Name

    Exp T

        Appl M

        F

        Appl M

        P

        Appl M

        J

        Appl M

A page from Preston's *Syllabus Book* for the Entered Apprentice Degree, where it alludes to the Four Cardinal Virtues by their initials T, F, P, J. This copy once belonged to the famous "time immemorial" Lodge of Antiquity No. 2, of which Preston was a member.

Preston's usage has much in common with John Browne's *Masterkey Through all the Degrees of a Free-Masons Lodge* (1798), which presented the following enlarged explanation:

The Four Cardinal Virtues in Divinity

TEMPERANCE reminds us to refrain from such irregularities as indispose our mental faculties, pall our appetites, waste our time, bring on a train of dreadful diseases and occasion an expence beyond our incomes. Let us, therefore, Brothers, endeavour to retain health, wisdom and tranquillity of mind, by paying a strict attention to this valuable virtue Temperance, as its neglect might inadvertently lead us to

FORTITUDE is that upright firmness of the soul which enables us to resist temptation and to persevere with steadiness against nay attacks of perils, dangers or bodily infirmities, which so constantly attend mankind, for with reason it behoves us to fortify our minds with courage, patience and resolution against any sufferings that may befall us, whether from the immediate hand of the Almighty or the injuries we may sustain from wicked and designing men who might, by threats or persuasion, attempt to prevail upon us to

PRUDENCE is the true guide to human understanding and consists in judging and determining, with propriety, what is to be said or done upon all our occasions, what dangers we should endeavour to avoid and how to act in all difficulties. The means we should therefore use to accomplish so desirable an end is to behave in every circumstance of life, and in all companies, with decent decorum so as the gain esteem and, in order to promote our own happiness, is to do the utmost in our power for the benefit of mankind, according to the our circumstances, and the opportunity we enjoy, which will ever bring to my remembrance when I was.

JUSTICE is that virtue wherein the peace and tranquillity of society depends, the happiness if individuals and the certain enjoyment of all their possessions, and constitutes an exact and scrupulous regard to the rights of others, with a deliberate purpose to preserve them upon all occasions, sacred and inviolable. In consequence thereof it should be our constant duty to keep the desires of our hearts within the bounds, by being true to our friendships and promises, to be just in all our demands and dealings, and to observe a due moderation, even in our just resentments, in doing which we cannot forget.

Browne further added to his description the following:

Cardinal Virtues, further Explained

TEMPERANCE is that due restraint of our Passions and Affections, which render the Body tame and governable; and frees the Mind, from the allurements of Vice; the Tenets of which. This Virtue ought to be the practice of every Mason, as it teaches him to avoid Excess, or contracting any vicious or licentious Habits, that might unvarily lead him to betray his Trust; *which*

FORTITUDE is that noble and steady purpose of the Soul, equally distant from Rashness or Difficulty, when found necessary or expedient, and ought to be deeply impressed on the Breast of every Mason, as a Fence or Security, against any Attack, that might be made upon him, by Force or otherwise, to extort from him, any of those royal Secrets; *which*

PRUDENCE teaches us to regulate our Lives and Actions, according to the dictates of right Reason; being that habit of the mind, by which Men wisely judge, and prudentially determine on all Things relative to their present, as well as their future Happiness; and ought to be nicely attended to, in all strange or mixed Companies; never to let drop or slip the least Hint, whereby then Secrets of our royal Art, might be illegally obtained; *which*

JUSTICE is the boundary of Right, and constitutes the cement of civil Society. Without the exercise of this Virtue, universal Confusion would ensue; lawless Force would overcome the Principles of Equity, and social Intercourse no longer exist. And as Justice in a great measure constitutes the realm good Man, so it ought to be the perpetual Study of the accomplished Mason, never to deviate from the minutest Principle thereof....

Thomas Smith Webb, author of *The Freemason's Monitor or Illustrations of Masonry* (1797). From Charles T. McClenachan, *History of the Most Ancient and Honorable Fraternity of Free and Accepted Masons in New York* (New York: Grand Lodge, 1892), 2: frontispiece.

Thomas Smith Webb's ritual

An explanation similar to the above was adopted by Thomas Smith Webb (1771–1819), who is sometimes called the "father" of American Masonic ritual. In 1790 the nineteen-year-old Webb became a Freemason in New Hampshire, and he was destined to leave a lasting impact on the fraternity. In 1796 he received the degrees of

Pennsylvania's "Ancient York Rite" and immediately set out to improve them.[14] At the same time he worked to revise the three degrees of Craft Masonry. The revised Craft rituals are commonly called "Webb-form" or "Webb's model work." His ritual was largely based upon *Jachin and Boaz* (London, 1762), a supposed exposure of the Moderns Grand Lodge (the premiere Grand Lodge of England), with additional borrowings from the English rituals of William Preston[15] and John Brown. Webb taught his version to students who transcribed enciphered copies of the rituals after which they travelled the country while being paid to lecture in Masonic lodges.[16] Differences in surviving copies of these cipher books reveal that Webb continued to improve his ritual. His students, sometimes called "itinerant degree lecturers," helped to stabilize the ritual by demonstrating and promoting Webb's version. As Webb's ritual was adopted older ritual practices disappeared and were lost.[17]

To assist in the adoption of his ritual Webb published *The Free Masons' Monitor, or Illustrations of Masonry* (Albany, 1797), which was the country's first guidebook to the rituals of Freemasonry. In the second edition of the *Free Mason's Monitor* (1802) Webb made further improvements and modifications. The popularity of his book led to

---

[14] *Proceedings of the Grand Chapter of Royal Arch Masons, of the State of Wisconsin, at its Forty-sixth Annual Convention, held in the city of Milwaukee, February 18 and 19, A.D. 1896* (Milwaukee: Burdick, Armitage & Allen, 1896), 88. According to an address of Alfred F. Chapman, Webb received the Royal Arch Degree on May 18, 1796 in Philadelphia's Chapter No. 32. Pennsylvania Masons contended that Webb altered the rituals, rather than improving them. The pre-Webb rituals survived in French-speaking lodges in the Caribbean which were chartered by Pennsylvania. These earlier rituals are reprinted in Arturo de Hoyos, *Reprints of Rituals of Old Degrees* (Washington, DC: Scottish Rite Research Society, 2015)

[15] For an excellent study of Preston's influence, as well as a copy of his Craft rituals, see Colin Dyer, *William Preston and his Work* (London: Lewis Masonic, 1987)

[16] The first American Masonic cipher ritual (dated 1822) addresses the four cardinal virtues by referring the reader to the *Monitor*. See Arturo de Hoyos, *Daniel Parker's Masonic Tablet* (Washington, DC: Scottish Rite Research Society, 2019), 59–60

[17] What we know of pre-Webb ritual comes mostly from the testimony of former Masons. For example, Benjamin W. Case, a physician who was made a Mason in 1796, in Newport, Rhode Island, recalled that during the initiation of an Entered Apprentice Mason there was an attempt made "to frighten or alarm the candidate … by making noises, shuffling on the floor, throwing sticks down and directing the candidate to step high." He also noted that in the Master Mason Degree: "After the candidate has gone through the first part of the ceremonies he is taken out into the preparation room and clothed, during which time the lodge the lodge is darkened and a coffin introduced, and three persons placed by it wrapped in winding-sheets, and three small glimmering blue lights placed on the coffin; then he is brought back into the lodge so darkened, carried past the coffin, and as he passes the three persons exclaim, O Lord, must he die!" — Testimony of Benjamin W. Case, in *Report of the Committee Appointed by the General Assembly of the State of Rhode–Island and Providence Plantations to Investigate the Charges in Circulation Against Freemasonry and Masons in Said State: Together with the Official Documents and Testimony Relating to the Subject* (William Marshall, State Printer, 1832), 76, 86

imitators. In the same year that Webb died, his star pupil Jeremy Ladd Cross (1783–1860) published *The True Masonic Chart, or Hieroglyphic Monitor* (1819).[18] It borrowed heavily from Webb's *Monitor* but was greatly enhanced by the addition of engraved illustrations. Similar books by other authors soon followed. Today, the Webb-style work continues to enjoy popularity, and its basic form is used by most American grand lodges. Although Webb's dream of a uniform ritual was not achieved, a near uniformity of language exists in the exoteric portions of ritual preserved in the printed monitors, particularly in such cases as the explanation of the four cardinal virtues.

Webb's ritual is generally looked upon with favor, although in earlier times "those engaged in its dissemination [were] regarded as interlopers, in the larger number of the jurisdictions."[19] Pennsylvania Masonic historian Alfred Creigh noted, "innovations were introduced by Thos. S. Webb, who received these degrees in Philadelphia prior to 1802, and is styled the Father of American Masonry. By what authority he changed the work and ritual, we have not the means of knowing, except to build up for himself the reputation of a learned Mason."[20] In spite of the fact that many of Webb's modifications were adopted throughout most of the country, he was "regarded by ... *Pennsylvania* brethren as having been something of a charlatan."[21]

Albert Pike was also among those critical of Webb's work, stating that the latter "was profoundly ignorant of the ancient symbolism; of no reading in the Classics, knowing nothing in regard to the old philosophers and the old religions."[22] Pike further remarked that "Webb and [Jeremy Ladd] Cross, and the babblers of their school, have never rightly interpreted a single symbol. Their business has been the more completely to conceal the meaning of all, by leading thinkers and the thoughtless alike away from the truth, by false interpretations."[23] The

---

[18] Jeremy L. Cross, *The True Masonic Chart, or Hieroglyphic Monitor* (New Haven, CT: Flagg & Gray, 1819)

[19] "Report of Foreign Correspondence" [Indiana], in *Proceedings of the M.W. Grand Lodge of Free and Accepted Masons of the State of New Jersey* ... (Trenton, N.J.: MacCrellish & Quigley, 1898) 18, pt. 1:42

[20] Alfred Creigh, *History of the Knights Templar of the State of Pennsylvania from February 14th, A. D. 1794: A. O. 676 to November 13th, A. D. 1866: A. O. 748. A. O. E. P. 69. Prepared and Arranged from Original Papers Together with the Constitution, Decisions, Resolutions and Forms of the R. E. Grand Commandery of Pennsylvania* (Philadelphia: J. B. Lippencott, 1867), 28

[21] *Proceedings of the Grand Chapter of Royal Arch Masons, of the State of Wisconsin, at its Forty-sixth Annual Convention, held in the city of Milwaukee, February 18 and 19, A.D. 1896* (Milwaukee: Burdick, Armitage & Allen, 1896), 88

[22] Pike, *Esoterika* (2005), 82–3

[23] Pike, *Esoterika* (2005), 254

antidote, Pike believed, was to consult the Classics and other ancient sources. Thus, in the present book, he turns to Marcus Tullius Cicero's *De Officiis*, written in 44 BC. Known in English as the *Three Books of Offices, or Morals Duties*, "the first two are supposed to be chiefly derived from a lost work of Panætius, a Greek philosopher, who resided in Rome in the second century before Christ."[24] In Pike's view, Cicero's work provided a rational exploration of the utility of the four cardinal virtues for the individual, while it also considered their impact on larger society. For Pike, every aspect of Masonic ritual was intentional. Its liturgy and symbolism must preserve some ancient moral, philosophical, religious or scientific truth capable of ennobling and elevating the candidate's nature. To Pike, the deeper philosophical interpretations were essential and fundamental to the education of Masonic candidates, in order for them to fully benefit from the initiatory experience. Any action or instruction which did not endow the initiate with a beneficent result was immaterial, senseless or void. The practical purposes of Masonic initiation aimed at self-improvement and self-realization. Vapid and indistinct discourse, couched in language resembling noble sentiment, was self-defeating and unworthy of the Masonic experience. Pike believed in the *ne plus ultra* of initiation by providing engaging dramatic ritual and practical instruction which led to personal enlightenment and the discovery of truth. This, he believed, was "more light in Masonry."

Masonry in body and soul

Moving from a foundation of moral philosophy, with the four Cardinal Virtues, to the symbolism of a mathematical proposition was an easy turn for Pike. He saw no discontinuity in addressing under a single cover both the concrete and the abstract in what might otherwise appear as an arbitrary or disparate arrangement. This is because he viewed every aspect of ritual—whether physical movement or the contemplation of an image or object—as threads of uniform contrast and continuity which added dimension to and united the whole cloth. In Pike's philosophy Freemasonry possessed a body and a soul, the seen and the unseen, overt substance and covert symbolism. For him, exterior Masonry was the performance of duty, although its interior

---

[24] Cicero, *De Officii* 1.5, in Cyrus R. Edmonds, trans., *Cicero's Three Books of Offices, and Other Moral Duties: also his Cato Major, an Essay on Old Age; Laelius, an Essay on Friendship; Paradoxes; Scipio's Dream; and Letter to Quintus on the Duties of a Magistrate* (New York: Harper & Brothers, 1871), v. Hereinafter "Edmonds (1871)."

value lay in its power to reconcile man's two natures and bring them into dynamic equilibrium. He believed that by attentive and regular practice Freemasonry can reveal both the ability and means to inspire any good person, irrespective of origin, creed, or status, to advance from the square to the compasses, i.e., to achieve a habitual and gradual mastery over the "lower nature" until one prefers and strives to act within the greater good. This is, in part, actuated and motivated by intellectual convictions which are revelatory to the individual. Such convictions may result from insights gleaned by a study of symbolism.

It should be understood that the symbols of Masonry are twofold. First, there are the traditional and physical "working tools" of the Craft (square, compasses, plumb, level, etc.) and other physical objects, which are instructive and natural symbols for action and behavior. They may, for example, remind us to "square our actions" or "circumscribe our desires." In short, they require a performance of duty. But there are also working tools for the mind and spirit. These are symbols which may not necessarily have a material or physical existence, except in their application. They require a key or solution to unlock their mysteries which unveil insights into the nature of reality and/or the self. These symbols may be found in mathematics, in the sciences, in philosophy, or in religion. There is no guarantee that the solution will come to everyone, and even when discovered, their applications may differ. If the physical working tools inform us *what* to do, the spiritual tools may reveal *why*, and what underlies the former. They are like architectural plans which are the underlying "spiritual" framework which forms the true foundation of the physical structure. Their revelations, real and profound, are the springs of action which educate, elevate, guide and inspire. A symbol like the 47th problem of Euclid is but one such example.

The 47th Problem

In 1775 William Meeson commended his readers "to moralize the whole first book of Euclid," adding that "The 47th proposition of the first book of Euclid's elements of geometry, is the foundation of all masonry, of whatever materials or dimensions."[25] This begs the question, "How and why is the Pythagorean Theorem a symbol?" This is the dilemma which prompted Pike's study. The theorem possess well-

---

[25] William Meeson, *An Introduction to Free Masonry: For the Use of the Fraternity; and None Else. In Four Parts* (1775); reprinted in Róbert Péter and Cécile Révauger, eds., *British Freemasonry 1717–1813* (Routledge, 2016), vol. 1, pp. 135, 140

known applications in operative masonry (such as creating a perfect right angle), but did it also have symbolic value? If so, what was its true meaning? It has been observed that the simplicity of many symbols all but guarantees their survival and, it is also well known, that symbols often persist even when their original meanings have been lost.[26] Pike was aware of this and was moreover dissatisfied because, in the majority of American Masonic rituals, the 47th Proposition is presented in language similar to the following:

> The 47th problem of Euclid was an invention of our ancient friend and brother Pythagoras, who, in his travels through Asia, Africa, and Europe, was initiated into several orders of Priesthood, and raised to the sublime degree of Master Mason. This wise philosopher enriched his mind abundantly in a general knowledge of things, more especially in Geometry, or Masonry. On this subject he drew out many problems and theorems; and among the most distinguished he originated this, when in the joy of his heart, he exclaimed, EUREKA, meaning I HAVE FOUND IT; and upon the discovery, is said to have sacrificed a hecatomb.

The 47th Proposition appeared prominently in the frontispiece of the Rev. James Anderson's *The Constitutions of the Free-Masons* (1723), the first official publication of the premiere grand lodge of England. Set on the ground between the two principal persons is a representation of the theorem, beneath which is the Greek word εὕρηκα (heúrēka), meaning "I have found it." Anderson mistakenly believed that the word was exclaimed by Pythagoras which he discovered the theorem. Rather, Vitruvius wrote that Archimedes (ca. 287–ca. 212 B.C.E.) exclaimed the word when he discovered the principle of displacement. The confusion, which is still perpetuated in Masonic books, was addressed by Pike:

> When a man of intelligence, a scholar, is gravely told, by the *Book of the Lodge* of one of the great Masonic writers that the forty-seventh problem of Euclid, in his joy for the discovery whereof, Pythagoras cried out

---

[26] See Clement A. Miles, *Christmas in Ritual and Tradition: Christian and Pagan* (London: T. Fisher Unwin, 1912)

"eureka" and sacrificed an hundred oxen, "teaches us that Masons are great lovers of the arts and the sciences in general," the "explanation" of this symbol of nothing, is not calculated to produce in his mind any great admiration of Masonic symbolism.

And as it was not Pythagoras who cried "eureka," but Archimedes, centuries afterward, upon making quite a different discovery, his respect for the learning of those to whom we owe our current Masonic lectures is likely to be slightly diminished by this proof of their ignorance.[27]

In the second edition of his *Constitutions* (1738), Anderson added that Pythagoras "became, not only the Head of a new Religion of Patch Work but likewise of an *Academy* or *Lodge* of good *Geometrician*, to whom he communicated a Secret, viz. That amazing Proposition which is the Foundation of all Masonry, of whatever Materials or Dimensions, called by Masons his HEUREKA, because they think it was his own Invention."

Anderson's allusion to the "Academy or Lodge" refers to the Pythagorean School, or Society, which was founded in the Greek colony of Croton in the 6th century B.C. It's believed that some of his ideas were obtained while he studied with Egyptian priests, who taught him the fundamentals of geometry, as well as metaphysics. His school emphasized the importance of mathematics to understanding the nature of the universe. It also focused on metaphysis and music, and the school played an important part of the development of western philosophy and science. Pythagoras taught that there is a divine order to the universe which was expressed and understood by the harmony of numbers and music, and that mathematical ratios explained the harmony of music. He taught that the rules and precision of both served as models for moral and ethical behavior. His school also emphasized the importance of diet, and that humans needed to live in harmony with the universe, which could only be done by understanding the natural relationship which existed between all things.

---

[27] Pike, *Esoterika* (2005), p. 76

Frontispiece, James Anderson, *The Constitutions of the Free-Masons*
(1723)

The earliest known evidence for the "47th Problem of Euclid" aka the "Pythagorean Theorem" comes from a Babylonian clay table, known as *Plimpton 322*. Written in cuneiform script, it dates from around 1800 B.C. The tablet lists groups of integers which precisely match the Pythagorean Theorem. However, the importance of the theorem was popularized by Pythagoras, who lived during the sixth century, B.C. The theorem simply states that in any right-angled triangle, the square of the hypotenuse (longest side) is equal to the sum of the other two sides. As a formula, it is written $a^2+b^2=c^2$. In the following example the square of a to b is 16 (4x4), the square of b to c is 9 (3x3), and the square of the hypotenuse *a* to *c* is 25 (5x5), which is equal to the sum of the other two sides (16+9=25).

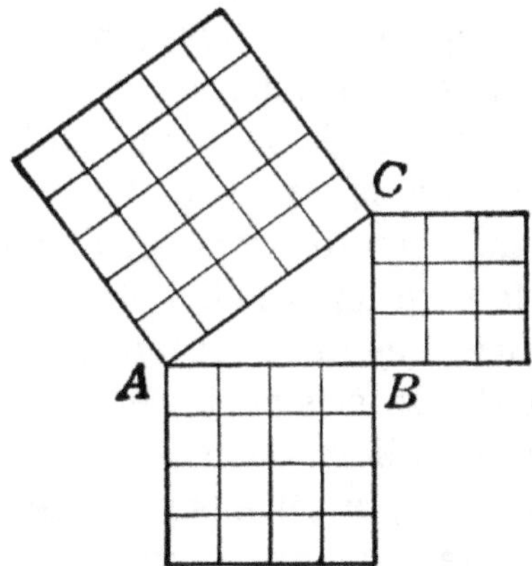

Around 300 B.C. Euclid's *Elements*, book 1, recorded the formula as Proposition 47, and it is also commonly called his 47th Problem. In operative masonry its well-known applications included creating perfectly square corners, as well as walls which were at a right angle to the ground. This could be achieved with the simplest of tools. A rope, repeatedly folded in half with knots tied at each fold in equal distances, was all that was necessary. One began by marking four units of measurement (*a* to *b* above); at the end of the last (*b*) a near-right angle measuring three units was approximated (*b* to *c*). Finally, by adjusting the measurement of hypotenuse to exactly five units between the starting and ending points (*a* to *c*) a perfect right angle is achieved. The simplicity, beauty, and utility of the theorem are self-evident.

Osiris, Isis and Horus

Was there a deeper symbolism to the 47th problem of Euclid? Plutarch believed so, and his interpretations still resonate with some students of esotericism. Plutarch of Chaeronea, Boeotia (not far from Delphi), was a Greek philosopher who lived in the 1st and 2d centuries. Well-known as a biographer and writer, he is believed to have written over 200 works. His teacher was Ammonius of Athens, an Egyptian who became a Platonic philosopher. Among Plutarch's works was his *Moralia*, which included his study *Of Isis and Osiris* (*De Iside et Osiride*), which assigned the three sides of the triangle to Egyptian gods:

One might conjecture that the Egyptians hold in high honour the most beautiful of the triangles, since they liken the nature of the Universe most closely to it, as Plato in the *Republic* seems to have made use of it in formulating his figure of marriage. This triangle has its upright of three units, its base of four, and its hypotenuse of five, whose power is equal to that of the other two sides. The upright, therefore, may be likened to the male, the base to the female, and the hypotenuse to the child of both, and so Osiris may be regarded as the origin, Isis as the recipient, and Horus as perfected result. Three is the first perfect odd number: four is a square whose side is the even number two; but five is in some ways like to its father, and in some ways like to its mother, being made up of three and two.[28]

In Plutarch's description Osiris is "active" since he ascends vertically, Isis is "passive" as she lies horizontally, and Horus mediates as their offspring, as the hypotenuse connects both. Plutarch's interpretation influenced several Masonic authors, although they have sometimes misremembered his remarks. For example, Albert G. Mackey wrote that "Among the Egyptians, it was the symbol of universal nature; the base representing Osiris, or the male principal; the perpendicular, Isis, or the female principal; and the hypotenuse, Horus, their son, or the product of the male and female principle."[29] Another writer, Frank C. Higgins, further complicated the error in his book *Ancient Freemasonry* (1923). In the illustration below he failed to position the triangle upright as Plutarch described, which further obscured the meaning.

---

[28] *De Iside et Osiride*, 56, Jeffrey Henderson, ed., *The Loeb Classical Library*; Frank Cole Babbit, trans., *Plutarch's Moralia in Sixteen Volumes. Moralia. Volume 5* (Cambridge: Harvard University Press, 1936), pp., 135–36

[29] Albert G. Mackey, "Triangle," *An Encyclopedia of Freemasonry and its Kindred Sciences* (Philadelphia: Moss & Co., 1874), p. 830.

From Frank C. Higgins, *Ancient Freemasonry* (1923)

Pike's earlier suppositions

Pike admitted his dissatisfaction with existing explanations of the Pythagorean Theorem. On September 8, 1888 he wrote of this to Robert F. Gould:

> I suppose that no one can say what symbols the English Lodges had before 1717 or with any approach to positiveness, whether they had any. Is there any information in regard to that?
>
> I am satisfied that part of the symbols after that in use, and still in use, came into Masonry from the hermetic books. Of the time of their introduction I have no information, but I think we may reasonably believe that until there were degrees in Masonry, there was not much symbolism. How could they have been used without degrees?
>
> If any of the symbols, for example, the compasses and square, were not the English school, this philosophy, I think, gave them its own meaning, leaving the old, single, rudimentary significations to continue for the mass of Masons. Is there, however, any *proof*, that *any* of them were used by Masons, in Scotland or England before 1717?

If the Hermetics introduced them, they knew what their symbolic meaning *then* was among the Adepts: but for some of them, older than Hermeticism, it had, no doubt, invented new meanings—*e.g.* for the numbers 3 and 4, making 7. Plutarch did not know what Pythagoras saw in the 47th Problem: and his explanation of it is but a conjecture.[30]

This was addressed in *Esoterika*, Lesson 5, where he dismissed Plutarch's notion as mistaken symbolism suggesting that he offered it because the true meaning behind the Egyptian Gods had been lost.[31]

Plutarch, who lived centuries after Pythagoras, in his *De Iside et Osiride*, endeavors to explain the 47th Problem, making the two sides forming the angle Osiris and Isis; and the hypotenuse, Horus.

But the explanation explains nothing. Why should Horus, the son of Osiris and his sister and wife Isis, be represented by the largest number, 5? Why should Osiris be represented by 4, and Isis by 3? No one knows, and Plutarch as little knew, what Osiris *was* and what Isis *was* to the Egyptians. When he wrote, all real knowledge about the inner meanings of the Egyptian Gods had long been lost. We can now read the inscriptions on the monuments of Egypt and we know a hundred times more about the Egyptian customs and manners than Plutarch did; but we know really little or nothing about their religion. We know that they had a great number of Gods; but we do not know what they represented or were; and the monuments do even lift a corner of the veil.

That the right-angled triangle did *not* represent Osiris, Isis and Horus is conclusively demonstrable by a single suggestion—that any other triangle, equilateral, acute or obtuse angled, would represent them just as well. Two lines forming a right-angle do not fitly represent husband and wife or brother and sister; nor does the hypotenuse, larger than either, which connected

---

[30] Pike, *Esoterika* (2005), xxxi–xxxii

[31] For an insightful study of the symbolism of the Egyptian pantheon, see Jeremy Naydler, *Temple of the Cosmos: The Ancient Egyptian Experience of the Sacred* (Inner Traditions, 1996)

their ends, in any way represent their child or issue; nor have the number 3, 4, 5, and 7, any significance at all as applied to them.[32]

Pike's also addressed Plutarch's interpretation in his *Readings of the 32°*:

Perhaps there is no symbol in Masonry for whose presence among our emblems it has been found so difficult to account, and which has been so persistently let alone, as the 47th Problem of Euclid, which figures in all our Monitors, as much out of place as an Etruscan cornice-stone in a Roman hovel. *We* know its meaning now, but Plutarch did not, nor did Iamblichus. It had been lost long before they lived. Pythagoras had too carefully concealed it; and these later writers looked in the wrong direction for it. Plutarch's explanation, altogether wrong, is as follows.

*   *   *

It is said that when Pythagoras discovered the 47th Theorem of Euclid, he sacrificed a *hecatomb* for joy. A ἑκατόμβη was strictly an offering of a hundred oxen; but even in Homer it had lost its etymological signification and signified only a great public sacrifice. We find in the *Iliad* mention made of a hecatomb of *twelve* oxen, and of hecatombs of sheep.

This theorem is, that in every right-angled triangle, the sum of the squares of the lengths of the base and perpendicular is equal to the square of the length of the hypotenuse.

As a mere mathematical theorem or proposition, this is of no especial importance, and has no special significance. Its principal *practical* use is, that if one erects a perpendicular line upon a base line, making one three measures and the other four, he will have one at an exact right angle with the other, if he connects the ends by a line of five measures. As a theorem it has no philosophical or religious value. To give it such a value, it must be in some manner a symbol. Pythagoras could not

---

[32] Pike, *Esoterika* (2005), 199

have so greatly exulted at discovering, if he did discover, this mere mathematical theorem, how ever valuable the knowledge of such theorems then may have been. There were fifty others equally as valuable.

He must have discovered in it and in the figure and numbers representing it, a new symbol, unknown or unnoticed before, of some ancient and valuable, truth or doctrine. To be able to add another symbol to those already known and used by the Sages who possessed the truth or doctrine, was worth a public sacrifice. Plutarch, supposing that Pythagoras brought his doctrine and its symbols from Egypt, wrote the whole treatise *Peri Isidos kai Osiridos* [*Of Isis and Osiris*] on that theory. He says that the base, of 3 measures, meant Isis, and the perpendicular, of 4, Osiris. But why these numbers should represent them, it was not in his power to explain, otherwise than by saying that the hypotenuse represented Horus, their issue, and if it measures 5, the other sides must measure 3 and 4. Why should Horus, the issue, measure 5, excelling by so much his father, Osiris? Certainly, he gives no reason for this, and there could be none. The *religious* explanation, according to Plutarch's interpretation, would be, Horus is equal to the squares of Osiris and Isis, added together. According to his explanation, the symbol taught no doctrine whatever, and was not in any sense mysterious. Other and much more apt symbols would represent Father, Mother, and Child or Issue.

Plutarch, like Iamblichus, was utterly ignorant of the meaning of what Pythagoras taught as to numbers. None of the scholars now know what he meant and they never will, while they look to Egypt or to books written long after his death for the explanation. He did *not* mean that the Deity created by the instrumentality of, abstract numbers.

But this figure *was* connected with his theories as to numbers, and in fact, its whole meaning consists in the numbers 3, 4, and 5, which the side of the triangle represent and measure.

Be that as it may, Pike's last interpretations, which follow below, present his most reasoned and coherent statements on these topics.

The Four Cardinal Masonic Virtues

The 47th Problem

The Four
CARDINAL MASONIC
Virtues.
The 47th. Problem.
III + IV = VII.

The
FOUR
Cardinal Virtues.

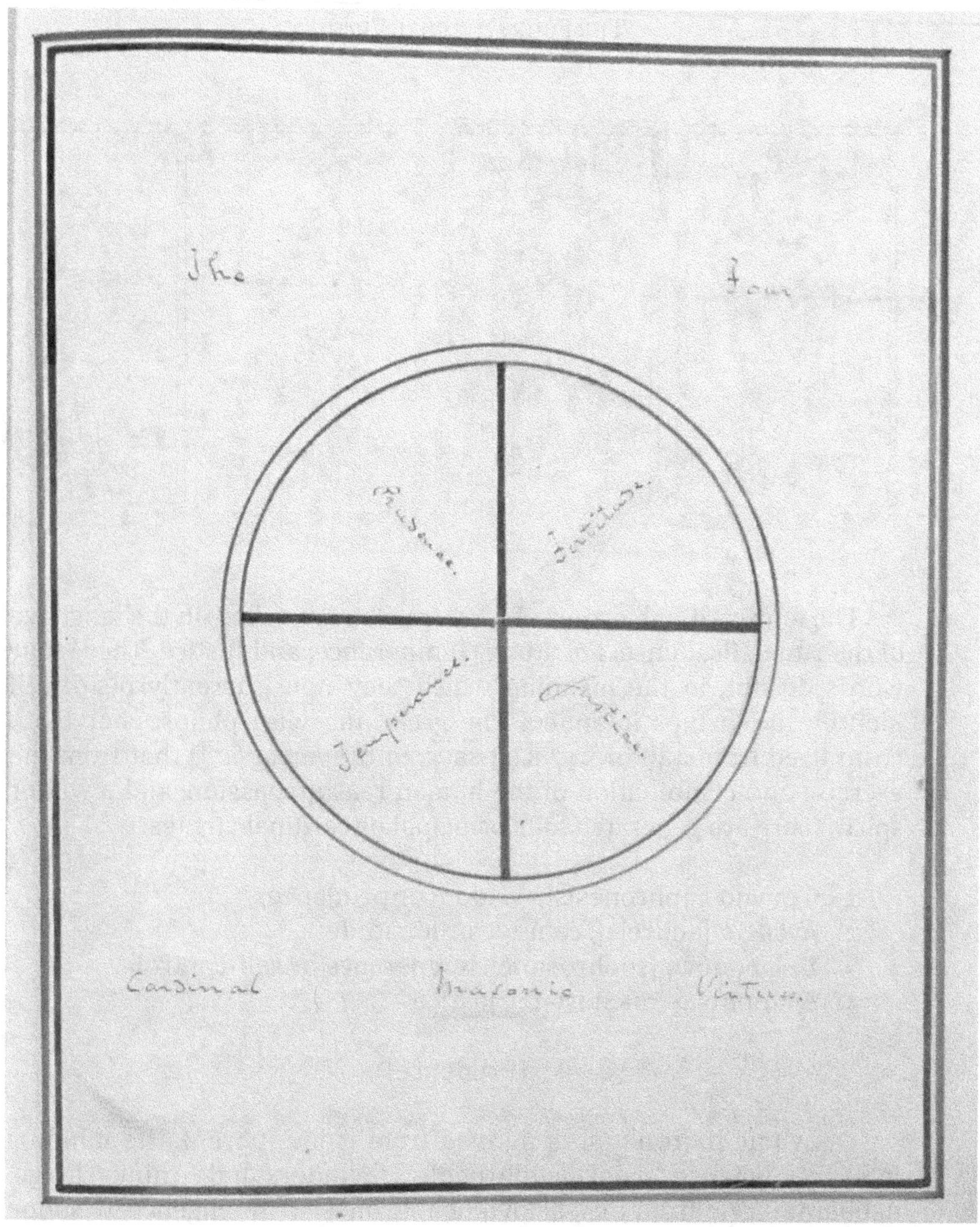

The
four
Prudence
Fortitude
Temperance
Justice
Cardinal Masonic Virtues

THE FOUR CARDINAL VIRTUES

The four cardinal virtues of a Freemason are called, in the language of the ritual, Prudence, Fortitude, Temperance, and Justice. These four words do not, in the meaning which they now currently bear, well identify the virtues intended. The great and wise philosopher Plato (who lived from 429 to 347 B.C.) says, in the *Republic*,[33] that from the exercise and combination of the human reason, passion, and a will or spirit, there are generated four principal or cardinal virtues:

1°, Φρόνησις |phronésis|, wisdom or prudence;
2°, Ανδρεία |andreia|, courage or fortitude;
3°, Σωφροσύνη |sóphrosuné|, temperance or self-control;
4°, Δικαιοσύνη |dikaiosynē|, justice.

[Prudence]

Φρόνησις |phronésis| is derived from φρήν |phrén|, the mind or intellect, whence φροέω |phroéo|, "I understand, think, judge, deliberate," and from this, φρόνησις |phronésis|, intelligence, wisdom, prudence, thoughtfulness, sagacity.

It is quite possible to disconnect all idea of virtue from each of these words. A man may be intelligent, of good understanding, thoughtful, judicious, deliberate, wise in some senses, very prudent, thoughtful and

---

[33] Plato, *The Republic* 4.247

sagacious, an yet not by any means virtuous; for all these are, in our modern English acceptance of the words, of the field of the intellect, and not of that of morality.

The word *prudence* is particularly ill-chosen. Undoubtedly, the virtuous man is the only truly wise man; but the word *prudence* is not now the equivalent of the word "wisdom." It rather indicates selfishness, and prudence of a quality of human nature that may certain consist with selfishness, un-generosity, want of sympathy, and a disposition to grasp, overreach, oppress and defraud, and a coward, like a forger or a thief, may be unimpeachably prudent.

The common meanings of *prudence*, now, are cautious, judicious pre-thought, circumspection, avoid of error, excess or danger. Very prudent men may, because of their prudence, be very false to friend or country; and to speak the truth maybe, as to offend a tyrant or the populace, defend the right, or endeavor to right the wronged or relieve the oppressed, always is, exceedingly imprudent.

Prudence may thus coexist in great perfection, with very contemptible traits of character, and in very base and sordid natures; may even aggravate these vices of character and nature, and aid them to make one more despicably selfish and unfeeling and even grossly vicious and immoral. For one may be very prudent in his sins and debauches; and very small souls are often very prudent ones.

The word *prudence* is from the Latin adjective *prudens*, a contracted form of *pro-videns*, which is from the compound verb *pro-vides*, "[to] see before, ahead of, or in front of one's self"; *video, videre*, meaning "I see, to see"; and the original meaning of *pro* being "before, in front of." Whence *prodvidere* came to mean to act with foresight, to take care, to look after or care for, to provide or make provision or preparation, to foresee, to see earlier. And *prudential* mean a pre-seeing, acquaintance with a thing, knowledge, skill, sagacity, good sense, intelligence, prudence, practical judgment, discretion.

Cicero, a scholar, philosopher and gentleman, often speaks of this virtue. Thus he says, "Id enim est sapientis, providere; ex quo sapientia *est* appellate prudentia" (It is a character of a wise man to foresee; whence wisdom is called prudence). —*Fragmenta*, apud Nonnum, 41.31.

"Prudentia ... constat ex scientia rerum bonarum et malarum et nec bonarum nec malarum" (Prudence consists in the knowledge of things good and evil, and neither good nor evil). —*De Natura Deorum* 3.15.

"Prudentia cernatur in delectu bonorum et malorum" (Prudence is displayed in the choice between good and evil things). —*De Finibus* 5.23.

"Ut medicina valetudinis sic vivendi ars est prudential" (As medicine is the art of health, so prudence is the art of living). —*De Fin|ibus|* 5.6.

"Civilis prudential," statesmanship;[34] *Prudens*, like *juris peritus*, "one skilled in the law"; *juris-prudentia*, "the science of law"; Prudence very rarely in the Latin meant cautious and circumspect.

|FORTITUDE|

Ανδρεία |andreia|, from Ανήρ, "a man," *vir*, meant primarily, "manliness, virility"; as the Latin *virtus* did, from *vir*, "a man"; whence courage, fortitude, bravery. In the present meanings of these words, the worst of men may be brave, courageous, and possessed of fortitude, whether in danger or pain. And in these qualities, the game-cock, hill dog, and horse may excel the best of men. An American Indian has abundant fortitude, which many of fine intellect and pure life have had very little. Alva[35] had courage, and the debauched Cavaliers and intolerant Roundheads[36] had it alike. It is a quality greatly valued and above measure honored; but in its common acceptance it is no virtue. Very fearless men, intrepid in all dangers, and of the utmost fortitude to endure torture, may be very bad men.

---

[34] The three preceding paragraphs were extracted by Pike from Wilhelm Freund, *Wörterbuch der lateinischen Sprache nach historisch-genetischen Principien, mit steter Berücksichtigung der Grammatik, Synonymik und Alterthumskunde. Nebst mehreren Beilagen linguistischen und archäologischen Inhalts* (Leipzig: Hahn, 1845), 3:1076–77

[35] *Alva.* Fernando Álvarez de Toledo y Pimentel, 3d Duke of Alba (1507–82), was the Spanish governor of the Netherlands, sent by Philip II of Spain to restore order to that country. Known as the "Iron Duke," for the manner in which he exercised his powers, it is believed that as many as 18,000 suffered tortures or hanging. A fearless leader and brilliant military strategist, he was later sent to conquer Portugal, which he accomplished.

[36] *Cavaliers and Roundheads.* During the English Civil War (1642–51) the Cavaliers were Royalists who supported King Charles I and the throne, while the Roundheads were the Parliamentarians, who opposed the "divine right of kings" and sought to make Parliament the supreme administrative authority. Perhaps the most renowned of the Roundheads was Oliver Cromwell, "Lord Protector of the Commonwealth of England, Scotland and Ireland" who abolished the monarchy.

|Temperance|

Σωφροσύνη |sóphrosuné| is from σῶφρον |sóphrón|, "of sound mind, prudent, wise, modest, temperate, sober, decent, upright, chaste, from σῶς |sōs|, *sanus*, sound, healthy, sane, and φρήν |phrēn|, "mind." It means not only temperance, but decency, modesty, sanity, sobriety, etc.

Cicero says, "Temperans quem Graeci Σώφρονα |sōphrona| appellant eamque virtutem σωφροσύνην [sōphrosynēn] vocant, quam soleo equidem tum temperantiam, tum moderationem appellare, nonnunquam etiam modestiam" (Temperance, which the Greeks call Sōphrona, and that virtue Sōphrosūnēn, which I am wont sometimes to call Temperance, sometimes Moderation, and sometimes Modesty). (*Tusc|ulanæ| Quæst|iones|* 3.8.16)

"Quæ (virtutis vis) moderandis cupiditatibus regendisque animi motibus laudatur, ejus est munus in agendo, cui temperantiæ nomen est" (Which potency |of virtue| in moderating the desires and regulating the impulses of the mind, has its promise in action, whose name is Temperance). (*Partitiones Oratoriæ* 22.66)

"Temperantia est quæ in rebus aut expetendis aut fugiendis ut rationem sequamur monet" (Temperance is that which admonishes us to obey reason in seeking or avoiding things). (*De Finibus* 1.14.47)[37]

As Temperance had several meanings, all derived from its primary meaning, which, from *tempus*, "a piece cut off, a part, portion," was "to divide"; whence, "to proportion only, to properly continue or compound, to mingle in the proportion, to soften, qualify, temper," etc. Thence, "to rule, regulate, manage, govern, order, to time, to string, to mend (or pen), to observe proper measure, moderate or restrain one's self, forbear, abstain, be moderate or temperate," so *virtus*, originally "manliness," had the various meanings of "strength, vigor, courage, openness, which excellence, goodness, value, power, moral perfection, bravery, gallantry," etc. And *fortitude* was from *fortis*, "strong, powerful"; from *fero*, "bear, endure"; and had the meanings of "strength, power, firmness, manliness, resolution, fortitude, bravery, courage, intrepidity."

Cicero says, "Magnitudinis animi et fortitudinis [proprium] est, nihil extimescere, omnia humana despicere, nihil, quod homini accidere possit, intolerandum putare" (What constitutes magnanimity and

---

[37] The four preceding paragraphs were extracted Wilhelm Freund, *Wörterbuch der lateinischen Sprache* (Leipzig: Hahn, 1840), 4:697–98

fortitude is, to fear nothing, to condemn all human affairs, and to think nothing intolerable that can happen to a man). (*De Off[iciis]* 3.27.100)[38]

[Justice]

Δικαιοσύνη [dikaiosynē] is the word that in the New Testament is constantly translated "righteousness." It had a much wider meaning than, in our modern acceptation, "justice" has. Δίκη [51ffe] was, properly *jus*, "law" (νόμος [nomos] being *Lex*, and δεμίς [demis], *fas*, "right"), also a right or a title. Thence δίκαιος [díkaios], "just, equitable, worthy, innocent, upright, righteous"; and thence δικαιοσύνη [dikaiosynē], "justice, equity, uprightness, righteousness."

Δίκη [51ffe] also means "a cause, judication, penalty, punishment, vengeance," and also "a custom."

Our word "justice" is from the Latin *justitia*, itself from the adjective *Justus*, this from *jus*, which is an abbreviation of *jussum*, from *jubeo*, a form of *jusso*, and which means, "I order, bid, tell, command, decree," etc., *jussus* being the participle. *Jus*, "what is commanded," mean "law, right, justice, judgment." *Justus*, "lawful, rightful, true," and in the plural, *justa*, "due ceremonies, formalities, funeral rites, obsequies," and *justitia* means "justice, right, right-wiseness, and righteousness."

Cicero says, "Quæ animi adfectio *suum* suum cuique tribuens atque hanc quam dico societatem coniunctionis humanae munifice et aeque tuens, iustitia dicitur, cui sunt adiunctae pietas, bonitas, liberalitas benignitas, comitas, quaeque sunt generis eiusdem." (That affection of the mind that gives to every one his due, and munificently and equally maintains this fellowship of human union of which I speak, is termed Justice, to which are adjoined dutifulness, kindness, benignity, amity, and whatever other qualities are of that same kind") (*De Finibus* 5.23)

And again, "Justitia erga Deos religio, erga parentes pietas, creditis in rebus fides ... nominatur" (Justice, with respect to the Gods, is termed religion; with respect to parents, dutifulness; and in matters of trust and confidence, good faith). (*Partitiones Orat[oriæ]* 22 *fin)*[39]

---

[38] Freund, *Wörterbuch* (1844), 2:642
[39] Freund, *Wörterbuch* (1844), 2:1205

Plato, from Raphael, *The School of Athens*

Plato, in his book styled Πολιτεια [Politeia], by the Romans *De Republicâ*, and by us *The Republic* or the *Commonwealth*, gives us the real or imaginary conversations of Σωκρατες, Sōkratĕs, with his friends and others, in regard, among other things, to these four virtues of a state and individual.

The virtues are also discussed in an earlier work, the *Protagoras*, Wisdom (Σοφία [sophia]), Justice (Δικαιοσύνη [dikaiosynē]), Courage (Ανδρεία [andreia]), Temperance (Σωφροσύνη [sōphrosynē]), and Holiness (ὀσιότης [hosiotes]). There, Sōkratĕs convinces Prōtagŏras that Justice and Holiness are nearly the same thing; and that temperance and Wisdom are one and the same. To be prudent (το σωφρονεῖν [to sophronein]) is to think well or rightly (εὖ φρονεῖν [en phronein]).[40] And the five, Wisdom, Temperance, Courage, Justice and Holiness, which are five names, belong to one and the same thing, Ἀρετὴ [arete], "virtue"; which word also means "probity, industry, fortitude,

---

[40] From phrén (φρήν), "mind." Hence, *phroneó* (φρονέω) means to "to think," "to be mindful," "to regard," "to have an opinion," etc.

integrity, power, strength," etc. And *arĕtĕ* is no doubt from the same root as the original name of the great race to which the Greeks, Romans, Persians and Indians belonged, and of which the Germans, Goths, Celts, Sclavs[41] and all the Latin and Saxon races are branches—*Arya*, or warrior, excellent, noble.

In *The Republic* 4.6 (428b[–428d]), Sōkratĕs says that a good State is wise, brave, temperate, and just (σοφή, ανδρεία, σώφρων, and δίκαία, [sophe, andreia, sōphrōn, dikaia]). First of all, he says, Wisdom holds in it a very auspicious place. A State is really wise, that is well advised. Nor are the sciences and arts and agriculture the things that make a State wise; but the good conduct of its foreign and domestic affairs, by the few who are its guardians and governors.

By the fortitude of a State he understands a firm and settled equanimity, in good or evil fortune, in danger and all untoward circumstances, made by the wisdom of the rulers to the habitual and indelible among the people; a constant maintenance of right and legitimate opinion, in regard to all things, whether alarming or seductive.

Temperance, he says, resembles a sort of symphony and harmony, more than Wisdom and Fortitude do. It is a certain decorum (κοσμος [cosmos], "order, discipline"), and restraint (εγκρατεια [egkrateia], "domination, superiority, control"), exercised over certain pleasures and desires; when the better and higher part of his nature governs the lower and so a State is temperate, when its better part governs it worse; and contemplate when the vicious and ignorant portion has dominion and sway. Fortitude and Wisdom reside in the few and not in the many; but Temperance makes the State temperate, anywhere it is diffused through the whole, making all to agree, upon some motive that inspires all, whether pride in the greatness of the State, pride of country, maternal interests, common lines, or other incentives, if not because all are prudent and wise. This concord is Temperance, a natural consent between the worse and better part, as to which of them is entitled to govern.

The principal parts of temperance are, he says, obedience of the governed to their governors; and that the governors themselves be temperate in drinking, feasting, and pleasures of love.

That one attends to his own affairs, and does not busy himself about those of others, or many things, this, Socrates said, is justice. The

---

[41] The Sclavs (also Sclaveni) were Slavic tribes of the Early Middle Ages, who settled in the Balkans.

proposition will sound strangely in modern ears. For now, for most part, while every one's own interest is the only God of his idolatry, every one deems it just and right to exercise a vigilant supervision over the morals and conduct, the life and fortunes of others, and a free press feeds the general appetite for gossip, news and libels in regard to the private concerns of all one's neighbors.

Nevertheless, Socrates and Plato thought that it seemed to be justice, to attend to one's own business. This justice, they said, enables temperance, fortitude and wisdom to have a being in the State, and to afford safety to it indwellers, as long as it continues therein.

"It would be difficult to determine," said Socrates,[42] "whether the coincidence of opinion between the governors and the governed, or the maintenance of legitimate opinion among the soldiers about what is to be dreaded, and what is not so—or what is wisdom and guardianship in the rulers—or whether this, by its existence in the State, makes it proportionally best—namely, when child and woman, bound and free, artificer, magistrate and subject, everyone, in short, attends to his own business, and does not meddle. With reference, then, to the virtue of the State, that power which makes each person in it attend to his own business, rivals its wisdom, temperance, and courage, justice is the habitual practice of one's own proper and special work." And it is justice that everyone should confine himself to that employment for which he is fit, every man, of each class, doing his own work and no other, in the State, and not adventuring upon that for which he is unfit; which, again, sounds strangely to us, among whom unfitness does not disqualify the ignorant and incompetent to legislate or judge or manage the finances or command armies; and the world for the most part, governs itself with as little wisdom as possible.

Each individual will be just, and do his own work, each part of whose soul does its own proper duty. The rational part should govern, as being wise, and charged with the care of the whole soul; and the spirited part (the passions of the mind, the will, etc.) should obey, and ally itself to the Reason.[43] The two, united, will control the concupiscent part, which in every one occupies the largest part of the soul, and by its

---

[42] Socrates, in Plato, *The Republic* 4.433c–433e

[43] Pike believed that two divine forces separated humans from mere animals, i.e., "the Moral Sense, whose conclusions are as absolute and infallible as those of the mathematics; by means of which Moral Sense, given in a greater or less degree to every man, he knows what is right and what is wrong for him to do," and "the Reason, which teaches man what is the wisest and best for him to do for his own good, and this also belongs in a greater or less degree to every man." See Pike, *Esoterika* (2005), 97–101

nature is insatiable of wealth; and they will take care lest, having acquired growth and strength by being filled with bodily pleasures, as they are termed, it becomes discontented with its own work, and so attempt to enslave and rule over those it ought not, and thus wholly upset the entire system of life. We call a man brave, when, through all the pains and pleasures of life, the spirit maintains the opinion dictated by Reason, about what is to be feared, and what is not. We call a man wise, from that small part of himself which governs him, and dictates this, inasmuch as it possesses the knowledge of what is expedient from each separately, and for the whole of the three together. And we call a man temperate, from the association and harmony of the principles, when the governing and the governed agree in one; when Reason governs, and the others are not in feud with it.

The man, of whose parts each one does its own appointed and fit will, of governing and obeying, will not embezzle, or violate a trust, or be guilty of sacrilege, theft or treachery, against individuals or the State; not be faithless to his oaths or other compacts; nor be guilty of adulteries, neglect of parents, or impiety against the Gods.[44] Justice, in the individual, is not to allow any principle in him to attempt what is the province of another, or to meddle and interfere with what does not belong to it. The just man well establishes his own affairs, and maintains proper self-government, keeping the order, becoming his own friend, and attaining and combining together his Reason (which includes his Moral Sense), his will and passions, and his concupiscent appetites, like the three musical strings, bass, tenor and treble; and out of the three to form one whole, temperate attuned, and able to perform whatever is to be done, either in acquiring wealth, or caring for the body, or managing any public or private affair bargain, in all these cases reckoning that action to be just and good, which always sustains and promotes this habit; and the knowledge that preside over this action, is Wisdom.

This harmony and correspondence, this one relation and subordination, among these things, the aggregate whereof is the soul, is the health of soul. It is Virtue. And Virtue is a kind of health, beauty and good habit of the soul, and vice its disease, deformity, and infirmity.

---

[44] *impiety against the Gods.* It is interesting that Pike makes this point, since both Socrates and Anaxagoras were executed for this offense. Specifically, Socrates was charged with not honoring the gods of the State, and of corrupting the youth of Athens. Plato's *Apology*, which records Socrates' defense, rather demonstrates the latter's devotion to the Oracle of Delphi, established by Apollo.

Justice is wisdom, and it is profitable. It is virtue and wisdom; and injustice is vice and folly, and never truly advantageous. It can have no true success, nor real power.

Of philosophy, continuing to pursue the idea that justice consists in every one doing his own work, and that fore which is best fitted, and in the due performance of its proper functions by each part of the human soul, Socrates said (and Masonry is philosophy, and so it is said of it also), that small talents do nothing great for any one, either private person or State; and that those who weary of and abandon the pursuit of philosophy, whose chief business was to devote themselves to it, and who, leaving it deserted and imperfect, lead thereafter lives neither becoming nor true, some are worthless, and others deserve punishment. For by their abandonment they make room and place for unworthy persons to intrude upon and disgrace philosophy, heaping upon her reproach and shame, and exposing her to the slurs and taunts of revilers.

For when the fit and competent will no longer do their proper work, other contemptible men, seeing the field unoccupied, and that dignities and honorable names follow the possession of it, like persons who from kennels and prisons take refuge in temples, these leap with alacrity from their low places and obscenity into philosophy.

Even in this portion of philosophy, he remaining dignity, in comparison with all the other arts, is still of impressive magnificence; which dignity many eagerly covet, who yet are of imperfect nature, and of words too narrow and souls too ignorant to comprehend even the nature of that unto which they thus imprudently thrust themselves. And when persons unworthy of instruction study philosophy, and meddle with it unworthily, the sentiments and opinions that come from them can be neither genuine, nor allow to true discretion or discrimination, but merely sophisms and dreary, tedious commonplaces.[45] From |*The Republic*|, 6.10, I quote literally, as follows, and it is very strikingly said:

> An extremely small number is left, said I, O Adimantus, of those who engage worthily in philosophy, men of that noble and well cultivated nature, which somehow seeks retirement, and naturally persists in

---

[45] ""And so when men unfit for culture approach philosophy and consort with her unworthily, what sort of ideas and opinions shall we say they beget? Will they not produce what may in very deed be fairly called sophisms, and nothing that is genuine or that partakes of true intelligence?" — Plato, *The Republic* 6.496a

philosophic study, through the absence of corrupting tendencies; or it may be, in a small State, some mighty soul arises, who has despised and wholly neglected civil honors; and there may be some small portion, perhaps, who having a naturally good disposition, hold other arts in just contempt, and then turn to philosophy ... and even of these few, they are such as taste and have tasted, how sweet and blessed is the acquisition of philosophy, and have withal sufficiently observed the madness of the multitude, and that none of them, as I may say, does what is wholesome in State matters, and that a man can get none of them to aid him in securely succumbing the just, but is like one falling among wild beasts, neither willing nor able to aid them in doing wrong, as one only against a host of wild creatures, and so without doing any good, either to the State, or his friends, perishes unprofitably to all the world. Quietly reasoning on all these things, and attending to his own affairs, like a man sheltered under a wall, in s storm of dust and foam borne along by the wind, by which he sees all about him overwhelmed in disorder, such an one is content anyhow to pass his life pure from injustice and unholy deeds, and to effect his exit hence with good hopes, cheerful and agreeable.[46]

These things, it is said in |*The Republic*|, 6, "Are good which make the brutal part of our nature most subject to the man, or rather, perhaps, to that which is divine; while those are evil which enslave the mild part of our nature to the brutal."[47] The compass is the symbol, to a Mason, of the one, and the square of the other.

In the *Laws* |5.6|, a temperate life is said to be "mild in all things, and exhibiting quiet pains and quiet pleasures, and loves not insane"; but the intemperate is said to be "Impetuous in all things, and exhibiting vehement pains, and vehement pleasures, and desires on the stretch and goaded on, and loves the maddest possible" and that "in a temperate life the pleasures exceed the pains; but in an intemperate

---

46 Plato, *The Republic* 6.496a–496e, in Henry Davis, *The Works of Plato. A New and Literal Version, Chiefly from the Text of the Stallbaum. Vol. II. Containing The Republic, Timæus, and Critias.* (London: Henry G. Bohn, 1849), 183–84

47 *The Republic* 9.12, in Davis, *The Works of Plato* (1849) 2:280

one the pains; but in an intemperate one the pains exceed the pleasures, in magnitude and intensity."[48]

Bust of Pythagoras in the Capitoline Museum, Rome

Pythagoras cultivated Temperance, and inculcated it upon his disciples. Iamblichus tells us that he required "abstinence from animal food, and also from certain foods calculated to produce intemperance,

---

[48] George Burges, *The Works of Plato. A New and Literal Version, Chiefly from the Text of the Stallbaum. Vol. V. The Laws.* (London: George Bell and Sons, 1880), 164

and to impede the vigilance and genuine energies of the reasoning power."[49]

Farther still, to this species the precept belongs, that sumptuous food should indeed be introduced in banquets, but should be sent away, and given to the servants, being placed on the table merely for the sake of punishing the desires ... And again, the exercise of taciturnity, and perfect silence, for the purpose of governing the tongue. Likewise a strenuous and assiduous resumption and investigation of the most difficult theorems. But on account of all these, we must refer to the same virtue abstinence from wine; paucity of food and sleep; an inartificial contempt of renown, wealth, and the like; a sincere reverence towards those to whom reverence is due, but an unfeigned similitude of behaviour and benevolence towards those of the same age; an animadversion and exhortation of those that are younger, without envy; and every thing else of the like kind.[50]

They knew that fortitude, according to the decision of right reason, is the science of things which are to be avoided and endured.[51]

With respect to the mind they were careful that they might not be at one time cheerful, and at another sad, but that they might be mildly joyful with uniformity. But they expelled rage, despondency, and perturbation.[52]

He performed that which appeared to him to he just, and which was dictated by right reason, not being diverted from his intention either by pleasure, or labor, or any other passion, or danger. His disciples also chose to die rather than transgress his mandates. And when

---

[49] Thomas Taylor, trans., *Iamblichus's Life of Pythagoras* (London: J.M. Watkins, 1818), ch. 31; p. 99
[50] Taylor, *Life of Pythagoras* (1818), ch. 31; p. 99
[51] Taylor, *Life of Pythagoras* (1818), ch. 31; p. 100
[52] Taylor, *Life of Pythagoras* (1818), ch. 31; p. 102

they were exposed to all various fortunes, they preserved invariably the same manners.[53]

That, however, which afforded them the greatest support in generous endurance, was the persuasion that no human casualties ought to be unexpected by men who are in the possession of intellect, but that all things ought to be expected by them, over which they have no absolute power.[54]

But if at any time they were in a rage, or oppressed with sorrow, or any thing else of this kind, they separated themselves from the rest of their associates, and each by himself alone; endeavoured to digest and heal the passion.[55]

No one of them when angry, either punished a servant, or admonished any free man, but each of them waited till his mind was restored to its former condition.[56]

They expelled from themselves lamentation, weeping, and every thing else of this kind; and that neither gain, nor desire, nor anger, nor ambition, nor any thing of a similar nature, became the cause of dissention among them.[57]

They thought that every one should pay the greatest deference to the laws and to his parents, and be obedient to them, not feignedly, but faithfully. And universally, they thought it necessary to believe, that nothing is a greater evil than anarchy; since the human race is naturally adapted to be saved, when no one rules over it[58] ... no man ought to be suffered to do whatever he pleases, but it is always necessary that there should be a certain

---

[53] Taylor, *Life of Pythagoras* (1818), ch. 32; p. 114
[54] Taylor, *Life of Pythagoras* (1818), ch. 32; p. 115
[55] Taylor, *Life of Pythagoras* (1818), ch. 31; p. 103
[56] Taylor, *Life of Pythagoras* (1818), ch. 31; p. 103
[57] Taylor, *Life of Pythagoras* (1818), ch. 31; p. 103
[58] Taylor, *Life of Pythagoras* (1818), ch. 30; p. 93 (with minor changes to the text)

inspection, and a legal a d elegantly formed government, to which each of the citizens is obedient. For the animal, when left to itself and neglected, rapidly degenerates into vice and depravity.[59]

They thought that, in determining what to do, they ought just to consider what duty and decency required; and after that, what would be advantageous and profitable. They looked to virtue as its own reward; and did what was right, because it *was* right to do.

Theages, the Pythagorean, said, "with respect to the virtues also, some are leaders, others are followers, and others are composed from these. And the leaders, indeed, are such as prudence; but the followers are such as fortitude and temperance; and the composites from these, are such as justice...."[60]

When the better part of the soul governs, but the less excellent part is governed; and the former leads, but the latter follows, and both consent, and are concordant with each other, then virtue and every good are generated in the whole soul. When likewise the appetitive follows the reasoning part of the soul, then Temperance is produced; but when this is the case with the irascible part, fortitude is produced; and when it takes place in all the parts of the soul, then justice is the result ... and justice is a certain established order of the apt conjunction of the parts of the soul and perfect and supreme virtue. In every good is contained in this; but the other goods of the soul cannot subsist without this... Justice contains the bond by which the whole and the universe are held together, and also by which Gods and men are connected ... JUSTICE is the supreme virtue. Hence virtue, when it consists in contemplating and judging, is called PRUDENCE; when in sustaining things of a dreadful nature, it is denominated FORTITUDE; when in restraining pleasure, TEMPERANCE; and when in abstaining from gain, and from injuring our neighbours, justice. [61]

---

[59] Taylor, *Life of Pythagoras* (1818), ch. 31; p. 105

[60] "From Theages in his Treatise on Virtues," in Taylor, *Iamblichus's Life of Pythagoras* (1818), 162

[61] "From Theages in his Treatise on Virtues," in Taylor, *Iamblichus's Life of Pythagoras* (1818), 169.

And Crito the Pythagorean said, "Prudence is the leader and mother of the other virtues. In all of them are co-harmonized and co-arranged with reference to the reason and law of this virtue."[62] Polus the Pythagorean, in his *Treatise on Justice*, said that it might

> ...be called the mother and the nurse of the other virtues; for without this a man can neither be temperate, nor brave, nor prudent. For it is the harmony and peace, in conjunction with elegance, of the whole soul. In the world therefore, it conducts the whole government of things, and is Providence, Harmony, and Law, by the decree of a certain genus of Gods. But in a city it is justly called peace, and equitable legislation; in a house, it is the concord between the husband and wife; the benevolence of the servant towards the master; and the anxious care of the master for the welfare of the servant. In the soul, it is the wisdom, which among men subsists from science and justice"[63] ... "and God is the principle, middle, and end, of all things which are accomplished according to justice and right reason.[64]

And Pythagoras said "that justice resembles that figure [the right-angled triangle], which is the only one among geometrical diagrams, that having indeed infinite compositions of figures, but dissimilarly disposed with reference to each other, yet has equal demonstrations of power."[65]

Plato divided the human mind into three parts:

1°—The rational or reasoning principle;

2°—The spirit or will;

3°—The appetite or passion, the last meaning only that vital impulse which leads from one sensation to another. The most excellent of these

---

[62] "From Crito in his Treatise on Prudence and Prosperity," in Taylor, *Iamblichus's Life of Pythagoras* (1818), 179

[63] "From Polus in his Treatise on Justice," in Taylor, *Iamblichus's Life of Pythagoras* (1818), 182

[64] "From Polus in his Treatise on Justice," in Taylor, *Iamblichus's Life of Pythagoras* (1818), 185

[65] Taylor, *Life of Pythagoras* (1818), p. 95. Taylor added, "Iamblichus here alludes to a right-angled triangle, and the Pythagoric theorem of 47. I of Euclid. For the square described on the longest side is equal to the two squares described on the two other sides. The longest side therefore is said by geometricians to be equal in power to the powers of the other sides."

faculties is Reason,[66] whose proper province is to direct and control the other faculties.

Intermediate between Reason and passion is the will or spirit, which should be an assistant to Reason in the pursuit of virtue, and should oppose the indulgence of base desires—all desires being legitimately under the control of the Reason and the will.

From the exercise and combination of these three faculties, are generated the four principal or cardinal virtues: virtue, he says, "whether exercised by individuals or communities, is one and the same, comprising, however, four parts: first, *Wisdom,* the essential qualification of rulers;—secondly, *Courage,* the property of the military class who defend the State;—thirdly, *Temperance,* the distinctive quality of a well-ordered and obedient commonalty; and, fourthly, *Justice,* by virtue of which each particular class or individual energises in his own sphere, without encroaching on that of his neighbours."[67] Justice is often used by Plato for virtue in general, because no action which is not also just, can be virtuous; and similarly with wisdom, temperance and balance.

The highest wisdom is that which enables man to distinguish unerringly between good and evil, and under all circumstances to prefer the good; and the highest courage is that which nerves and strengthens him always to be the soldier of that which is right, just and true. The one will cause him always to prefer the right and true to that which is expedient and may seem profitable; and the other enables him to brave public opinion and be unmoved even by ridicule. A wise and brave man will neither frown upon nor flatter the people or a tyrant, nor desert the weaker cause, if it be just, nor hold success to be better than merit; and what was said of Cato may always be said of him when the feeble or fallen cause is the just one: *victrix causa deis placuit, sed victa Catoni,*[68] |"The winning cause pleased the gods, but the losing cause pleased Cato"|.

A wise thoughtfulness is never the heritage of a base or bad man; and a calm and collected moral courage is never divorced from moral excellence. Temperance or self-control is the issue and, as it were, an outward manifestation, in practice and habit, of wisdom, and the chief

---

[66] "Reason ... teaches man what is the wisest and best for him to do for his own good, and this also belongs in a greater or less degree to every man.... It is the Reason, by the analogies perceived and formulated whereby we attain by observation of phenomena a knowledge of causes." Pike, *Esoterika* (2005), 97–98

[67] Davis, *The Works of* Plato [...] *Vol. II.* (1849), xxiv–xxv

[68] Lucan, *Pharsalia* 1.128

and head of all the virtues.[69] Injustice is not only wicked, but always unwise, a wrong to be repented of, and never other than a mistake and great unwisdom.

These virtues are much discussed by Aristotélēs, in his *Nicomachean Ethics.*[70]

The happy man, he says, "will always or most of all men, live in the practice and contemplation of virtuous actions, and he will bear the accidents of fortune most nobly, and in every case, and altogether suitably, as a man in reality good, and a faultless cube."[71]

"Some of the virtues he calls intellectual, and some moral. Wisdom and prudence are of the former; and temperance of the latter. We praise the wise man according to his habits; and praiseworthy habits are called virtues;"[72] so that wisdom is a virtue, though not a moral one. And on the other hand Cicero says *temperantia est scientia.*[73] The moral virtues are the children of the intellectual ones. A man is temperate because he is wise, prudent, discreet; and only a sound wisdom can, in many cases, teach us what is just. The science of the law consists in accurately defining, by nice and sound distinctions, what is just and right and equitable in given cases.

The virtues are naturally destroyed both by defect and excess. This holds good in the case of temperance and courage and all the other virtues.

> For he who flies from and is afraid of everything, and stands up against nothing, becomes a coward; and he who fears nothing at all, but goes boldly at everything, becomes rash. In like manner, he who indulges in the enjoyment of every pleasure, and refrains from none, is

---

[69] "Now, the men we live with are not perfect and ideally wise, but men who do very well, if there be found in them but the semblance of virtue. I therefore think that this is to be taken for granted, that no one should be entirely neglected who shows any trace of virtue; but the more a man is endowed with these finer virtues—temperance, self-control, and that very justice about which so much has already been said—the more he deserves to be favoured. I do not mention fortitude, for a courageous spirit in a man who has not attained perfection and ideal wisdom is generally too impetuous; it is those other virtues that seem more particularly to mark the good man." —Cicero, *De Officiis* 1.15.46

[70] The ten books of the *Nicomachean Ethics* were originally lectures delivered at the Lyceum, which were supposedly edited by Nicomachus, Aristotle's son.

[71] Aristotle, *Ethics* 1.10.7, in R[obert] W[illiam] Browne, *The Nicomachean Ethics of Aristotle* (London: George Bell and Sons, 1889), 24–27

[72] Aristotle, *Ethics* 1.13.15, in Browne, *Nicomachean Ethics of Aristotle* (1889), 32

[73] Browne, *Nicomachean Ethics of Aristotle* (1889), 33, fnt. a. "Temperance is knowledge" is a summation of Cicero's remarks in *De Officii* 3, not a direct quotation.

intemperate; but he who shuns, all, as clowns do, becomes a kind of insensible man. For temperance and courage are destroyed both by the 'excess and the defect, but are preserved by the medium.[74]

He who abstains from the bodily, and in this very thing takes pleasure, is temperate; but he who feels pain at it is intemperate; and he who meets dangers habits, and rejoices at it, or at least feels no pain, is brave; but he who feels pain is a coward; for moral virtue is conversant with pleasures and pains; for by reason of pleasure we do what is wicked, and through pain we abstain from honourable acts.[75]

In one way we call these things just which are adapted to produce and preserve happiness and its parts for the social community[76] ... And for this reason justice often appears to be the most excellent of the virtues; and neither the evening nor the morning star relatively is so admirable. And in a proverb we say, 'In justice all virtue is comprehended.'[77]

---

[74] Aristotle, *Ethics* 2.2.6–7, in Browne, *Nicomachean Ethics of Aristotle* (1889), 36. Browne concludes with "preserved by the mean."

[75] Aristotle, *Ethics* 2.3.1, in Browne, *Nicomachean Ethics of Aristotle* (1889), 37

[76] Aristotle, *Ethics* 5.1.11, in Browne, *Nicomachean Ethics of Aristotle* (1889), 119. Thomas Aquinas cited this passage in his *Summa Theologica*, 90.2.3, in answer to the query, "Whether the law is always directed to the common good?" He responded, "...the law belongs to that which is a principle of human acts, because it is their rule and measure. Now as reason is a principle of human acts, so in reason itself there is something which is the principle in respect of all the rest: wherefore to this principle chiefly and mainly law must needs be referred. Now the first principle in practical matters, which are the object of the practical reason, is the last end: and the last end of human life is bliss or happiness, as stated above.... Consequently the law must needs regard principally the relationship to happiness. Moreover, since every part is ordained to the whole, as imperfect to perfect; and since one man is a part of the perfect community, the law must needs regard properly the relationship to universal happiness. Wherefore the Philosopher, in the above definition of legal matters mentions both happiness and the body politic: for he says (Ethic. v, 1) that we call those legal matters 'just, which are adapted to produce and preserve happiness and its parts for the body politic': since the state is a perfect community, as he says in Polit. i, 1."

[77] Aristotle, *Ethics* 5.1.12, in Browne, *Nicomachean Ethics of Aristotle* (1889), 119. Regarding the statement "In justice all virtue is comprehended," Cicero, *Rhetorica ad Herrenium*, 3.2, notes, "Justice is equity, giving to each thing what it is entitled to in proportion to its worth." And in *De Partitione Oratoria*, 78, "Justice to the Gods is called *Religion*, to our Parents *Dutifulness*, and towards all Men *Benevolence*: In Things committed to our Trust, Justice is called *Fidelity*; in the Moderation of Chastisement, *Lenity*; and, where we bear a particular Good-will, it is named *Friendship*."

The following maxims, from various books of different ages, are worthy to be at all times had in consideration and remembrance by all Masons.

ON PRUDENCE
|REMARKS BY FRANCIS QUARLES|

Be not instable in thy resolutions, nor various in thy actions, nor inconstant in thy affections: so deliberate, that thou mayst resolve; so resolve, that thou mayst performe; so perforate, that thou mayst persevere: mutability is the badge of infirmity.[78]

Look well before thou leap into the chair of heaven: the higher thou climbest, the lower thou fallest: if vertue preferre thee, vertue will preserve thee; if gold or favour advance thee, thy honour is pinned upon the wheel of fortune: when the wheele shall turne, thy honour falls, and thou remainest an everlasting monument of thy own ambitious folly.[79]

Let not thy fancy be guided by thine eye; nor let thy will be governed by thy fancy: thine eye may be deceived in her object, and thy fancy may be deluded in her subject: let thy understanding moderate betweene thine eye, and thy fancy; and let thy judgement arbitrate between thy fancy and thy will; so shall thy fancy apprehend what is true: so shall thy will elect what is good.[80]

---

[78] Francis Quarles, *Enchiridion* (1641) 3.35
[79] Quarles, *Enchiridion* (1641) 2.72
[80] Quarles, *Enchiridion* (1641) 2.15

Francis Quarles (1592–1644), was an English prose-writer, poet, and chronologer who was once secretary to Archbishop James Usher. Quarles's most famous book, *Emblems* (1634) used symbolic images to teach scriptural lessons. Illustration from *The School of the Heart* (1808)

|Remarks by Plato and Socrates|

Plato, in *The Laws*, Book 1, ch. 6, says, "Now that which is the first good the leader of the divine, is prudence; but the second, after intellect, is a temperate habit of the soul; from these two combined with fortitude, the third in order will be justice; and the fourth is fortitude...."[81] He who has enacted the laws shall commit the execution of them all to some persons on account of their prudence, and to some who have a reputation of truthfulness; so that intellect, binding all these together, may exhibit them as following temperance and justice, and not wealth or ambition. And in Book 1, ch. 14:

> When we endeavour to render any one fearful in combination with justice, must we not cause him to overcome those, who are arrayed with, and previously exercised in, shamelessness, by his having contended with his own lusts; and by contending with and overcoming his usual mode of life, he must needs become perfect in fortitude; but whosoever is unexperienced and unexercised in contests of this kind, he will not become even the half of himself as regards virtue. But how will any one be perfectly temperate, who has not fought with, and overcome by reason, and labour, and art, in sport and in earnest, many pleasures and lusts, that urge him to act with shamelessness and injustice, but who is impassive with respect to all such things?[82]

In Book 2, ch. 5:

> On this account we say that the judges of these things stand in need of virtue; because they ought to be partakers of the rest of prudence and fortitude. For a true judge ought not to learn how to judge from a theatre, being stupefied by the clamours of the multitude, and by his own ignorance; nor on the other hand, while knowing, ought he through unmanliness and cowardice to give from the same mouth, with which when about to

---

81 Burges, *The Works of Plato. Vol. V. The Laws* (1880), 11
82 Burges, *The Works of Plato. Vol. V. The Laws* (1880), 37

judge, he called upon the Gods, a decision containing a falsehood, through a facile disposition.[83]

This is said of these whose duty it was to decide upon the excellence or demerit of the music of the theatre; and it is added that, "A judge does not sit as the disciple, but, as is just, the teacher rather of the spectators, and as about to oppose himself to those, who do not afford pleasure fitly and properly to the spectators."[84] And, undoubtedly, fortitude, firmness, and decision of character, are as necessary to every judge, as knowledge of the law. It is no worse in a judge to take bribes in money from a suitor, than to subordinate his judgment to the will or needs of a party, or to be bribed by the promise of popularity to register the edicts of the mob or of a faction. And those whose duty or business it is to lead and guide the people, the legislators, conductors of the press, and citizens to whom the people look for advice, are even more like the judges of the theatre; for the political sagacity and morality of the people, and their discrimination as to measures and man, are as defective and worthless as their musical taste. Wherefore the legislator, the editor, and the private citizen having experience, and whose intellect has caused him to profit and become wiser by his experience, have little manliness, and are little less than contemptible, if they are disciples and are not teachers of the restless, fickle, easily misled people, the spectators in the theatre of affairs. And when, through a facile and yielding disposition, a fear of offending what they call public opinion, they knowing the truth, teach falsehood instead, arrive at wrongs, and permit the canons of political morality and official decency to fall into contempt, this is unmanliness and cowardice and an admission of servile condition and a nature ready to cringe to a master, and is inconsistent with the character of a just and honest man.

In the *Gorgias*, Socrates says,

> This appears to me to be the mark to which we ought to look for the guidance of our life and referring all private and public actions to this point, that justice and temperance may be ever present with him who will be blessed, and to act accordingly; not suffering his desires to be intemperate, nor endeavoring to satisfy them; which is an irremediable evil, causing a man to live like a

---

83 Burges, *The Works of Plato. Vol. V. The Laws* (1880), 53–54
84 Burges, *The Works of Plato. Vol. V. The Laws* (1880), 54

robber. For such a one could neither be dear to any other man, nor to God; for it is impossible there can be any communion between them; and where there is no communion there can be no friendship. The sages, too, say, Callicles, that heaven and earth, gods and men, are held together by communion, friendship, order, temperance, and justice; and for this reason, my friend, they call this universe order,' and not disorder or intemperance.[85]

|REMARKS BY CICERO|

Cicero, the Roman scholar, philosopher, orator and gentleman, in his three books of *De Officii*, or of *Moral Duties*, written to his son Marcus, for his instruction, spoke at length of the four cardinal virtues. We shall not find a wiser teacher, as the extracts which follow will show.

Whatever is virtuous arises from some one of those four divisions: for it consists either in sagacity and the perception of truth; or in the preservation of human society, by giving to every man his due, and by observing the faith of contracts; or in the greatness and firmness of an elevated and unsubdued mind; or in observing order and regularity in all our words and in all our actions, in which consists moderation and temperance.[86]

1st, OF PRUDENCE

Though these four divisions are connected and interwoven with one another, yet certain kinds of duties arise from each of them. As, for instance, in that part which I first described, and under which I comprehended sagacity or wisdom, consists the search after and discovery of truth; and this is the characteristic function of that virtue: for the man who is most sagacious in discovering the real truth in any subject, and who can, with the greatest perspicacity and quickness, both see

---

85 Plato, *Gorgias*, 135–36, in Henry Cary, trans., *Select Dialogues of Plato: a New and Literal Version Chiefly from the Text of Stallbaum* (New York: Harper & Brothers, 1890), 231
86 Cicero, *De Officii* 1.5, in Edmonds (1871), 11

and explain the grounds of it, is justly esteemed a man of the greatest understanding and discernment. From hence it follows that truth is, as it were, the subject-matter which this faculty handles, and on which it employs itself. As to the other three virtues, they necessarily consist in acquiring and preserving those things with which the conduct of life is connected, in order to preserve the community and relations of mankind, and to display that excellence and greatness of soul which exhibits itself as well in acquiring resources and advantages both for ourselves and for our friends, as, still more conspicuously, in properly disregarding them. As to order, resolution, moderation, and the like, they come into that rank of virtues which require not only an operation of the mind, but a certain degree of personal activity; for it is in observing order and moderation in those things which constitute the objects of active life, that we shall preserve virtue and decency.[87]

Now, of the four divisions under which I have ranged the nature and essence of virtue, that which consists in the knowledge of truth principally affects the nature of man. For all of us are impelled and carried along to the love of knowledge and learning, in which we account it glorious to excel, but consider every slip, mistake, ignorance, and deception in it, to be hurtful and shameful. In this pursuit, which is both natural and virtuous, two faults are to be avoided. The first is, the regarding things which we do not know as if they were understood by us, and thence rashly giving them our assent. And he that wishes, as every man ought to wish, to avoid this error, must devote both his time and his industry to the study of things. The other fault is, that some people bestow too much study and pains upon things that are obscure, difficult, and even immaterial in themselves. When those faults are avoided, all the pains and care a man bestows upon studies that are virtuous in themselves, and worthy of his knowledge, will be deservedly commended. ...All our thoughts, and every

---

[87] Cicero, *De Officii* 1.5, in Edmonds (1871), 12

motion of the mind, should be devoted either to the forming of plans for virtuous actions, and such as belong to a good and happy life, or else to the pursuits of science and knowledge. I have now treated of at least the first source of duty.[88]

2d, OF JUSTICE

Now, as to the other three, the most extensive system is that by which the mutual society of mankind, and, as it were, the intercourse of life, is preserved. Of this there are two parts: justice, in which virtue displays itself with the most distinguished luster, and from which men are termed good; and allied to this, beneficence, which may likewise be termed benevolence, or liberality. Now, the chief province of justice is, that no person injure another, unless he is provoked by suffering wrong; next, that public property be appropriated to public, and private to individual, use.[89]

Which maxim deserves to be much more largely developed, as, for example, by showing how supreme an injustice it is in a Republic to appropriate to itself the means of its citizens and wards by holding and using what it owes them, by employing and paying attorneys and officers to impede the allowances of just claims; by establishing tribunals to deny justice, and by evasions and delays making its tardy justice of little worth. So unjust and unequal taxes and assessments levied upon industry for the benefit of idle wealth, or to oppress one portion of the country in order to enrich another, and the giving of public moneys or public property to individuals or associations all violate the great principle that public property is to be appropriated to public use only, and private property to individual use.

But, as has been strikingly said by Plato, we are not born for ourselves alone, and our country claims her share, and our friends their share of us; and, as the Stoics hold, all that the earth produces is created for the use of man, so men are created for the sake of men, that they

---

[88] Cicero, *De Officii* 1.6, in Edmonds (1871), 12–13
[89] Cicero, *De Officii* 1.7, in Edmonds (1871), 13–14

may mutually do good to one another; in this we ought to take nature for our guide, to throw into the public stock the offices of general utility by a reciprocation of duties; sometimes by receiving, sometimes by giving, and sometimes to cement human society by arts, by industry, and by our resources.[90]

Now the foundation of justice is faithfulness, which is a perseverance and truth in all our declarations and in all our promises.... There are two kinds of injustice; the first is of those who offer an injury, the second of those who have it in their power to avert an injury from those to whom it is offered, and yet do it not.... Those wrongs which are inflicted for the very purpose of doing an injury, often proceed from fear; as for instance, when a man who is contriving to injure another is afraid, unless he executes what he is meditating, that he may himself sustain some disadvantage; but the great incentive to doing wrong is to obtain what one desires, and in this crime avarice is the most pervading motive.... But the main cause why most men are led to a forgetfulness of justice is their falling into a violent ambition after empire, honors, and glory.... What is deplorable in this matter is, that the desire after honor, empire, power, and glory, is generally most prevalent in the greatest soul and the most exalted genius for which reason every crime of that sort is the more carefully to be guarded against.[91]

Various are the causes of men omitting the defense of others, or neglecting their duty toward them. They are either unwilling to encounter enmity, toil, or expense; or, perhaps, they do it through negligence, listlessness, or laziness; or they are so embarrassed in certain studies and pursuits, that they suffer those they ought to protect to be neglected. Hence we must take care lest Plato's observation with respect to philosophers should be falsified: "That they are men of integrity, because they are solely engaged in the pursuit of truth, and despise and

---

[90] Cicero, *De Officii* 1.7, in Edmonds (1871), 14–15
[91] Cicero, *De Officii* 1.7, 8, in Edmonds (1871), 15–16

neglect those considerations which others value, and which mankind are wont to contend for among themselves." For, while they abstain from hurting any by the infliction of injury, they indeed assert one species of honesty or justice, but they fail in another; because, being entangled in the pursuits of learning, they abandon those they ought to protect. Some, therefore, think that they would have no concern with the government unless they were forced to it; but still, it would be more just that it should be done voluntarily; for an action which is intrinsically right is only morally good in so far as it is voluntary.[92]

There are others who, either from a desire to improve their private fortune, or from some personal resentments, pretend that they mind their own affairs only that they may appear not to do wrong to another. Now such persons are free from one kind of injustice, but fall into another; because they abandon the fellowship of life by employing in it none of their zeal, none of their labor, none of their abilities.

To concern ourselves in other people's affairs is a delicate matter. Yet Chrēmēs, a character in Terence,[93] thinks, that there is nothing which has a relation to mankind in which he has not a concern [*Homo sum: humani nihil a me alienum puto*[94]]. Meanwhile, because we have the quicker perception and sensation of whatever happens favorably or untowardly to ourselves than to others, which we see as it were at a greater

---

[92] Cicero, *De Officii* 1.9, in Edmonds (1871), 16–17

[93] *Terence*, or Publius Terentius Afer (195/185–159 BC), was a Roman playwright. His birth date is disputed.

[94] "I am a human; I consider nothing that is human alien to me." —Terence, *Heauton Timorumenos*, Act I., Sc. 1. Appended to the reference, Edmonds notes, "Augustin, who was made bishop of Hippo, A.D. 395, mentions the universal applause with which this admirable sentiment was received in the theater. He himself has left us an expression of the same idea in the following words: *Omnis homo est omni homini proxinras, nee ulla cogitanda est longinquitas generis ubi est natura communis.* 'Every man is most closely connected with his every fellow man, nor should any distance of relationship enter into consideration where there is a common nature.'"

Pike modified the remark to express his interests, stating, "I am a Mason and nothing that concerns Masonry is uninteresting to me." —Weldon B. White, "Albert Pike Memorial Service," in *Transactions of The Supreme Council, 33°* (Washington, D.C.: The Supreme Council, 1965), 352

distance, the judgment we form of them is very different from what we form of ourselves. Those therefore are wise monitors who teach us to do nothing of which we are doubtful, whether it is honest or unjust; for whatever is honest manifests itself by its own luster, but doubt implies the entertainment of injustice.[95]

You are not to perform those promises which may be prejudicial to the party to whom you promise, nor if they may be more hurtful to you than they can be serviceable to him. [And still more, those that are contrary to some higher duty to your fellows, friend, family, city or state, or to God.] It is inconsistent with our duty that the greater obligation should be postponed to the less.[96]

If you swear to keep the secrets of a brother, you can keep no other than his lawful secrets. If he confides it to you that he has committed forgery, robbery, rape, or arson, or violated a trust, a higher duty to society, the state and law, requires you to make it known. You cannot, knowing him to have committed a felony, conceal it to shield him, without becoming his accomplice and accessory after the fact, being false to your duty as a citizen, a violator of the law of the land, and a criminal, and an enemy of public order and the public morals. As to murder and treason, it never can be at your option whether you shall denounce the criminal or commit a crime by shielding him.[97]

"The rigor of the law is the rigor of injustice," is a saying that has now passed into a proverb.[98] Whence it may often be unjust, as it is often heartless and cruel, to insist upon full measure of one's legal rights. It is often the act of a dishonorable knave to interpose the plea of prescription, as it is to enforce promises that are onerous for the maker and were wrung from his hand by necessity. The edicts of the Prætor[99] cancelled many such promises; and because injustice was of

---

[95] Cicero, *De Officii* 1.9, in Edmonds (1871), 17–18

[96] Cicero, *De Officii* 1.10, in Edmonds (1871), 18

[97] Pike makes a similar point when discussing the 4° Secret Master, "The secrets of our brother, when communicated to us, must be sacred, if they be such as the law of our country warrants us to keep. We are required to keep none other, when the law that we are called on to obey is indeed a law, by having emanated from the only source of power, the People." (Arturo de Hoyos, *Morals and Dogma: Annotated Edition* 2d ed. [Washington, DC: Supreme Council, 33°, 2011], 4:12)

[98] Cicero, *De Officii* 1.10, in Edmonds (1871), 19

[99] *Prætor*. An elected magistrate in ancient Rome.

so common occurrence in the strict enforcement of legal rights, the jurisdiction of the Court of Equity grew up, and cases were held to be lacking by performance, out of the Statute of Frauds, to the end that a Statute enacted to prevent fraud, might not become the fruitful mother of fraud. For the same reason, redemption of lands mortgaged was allowed, after the title was by strict law and the letter of contract lost to the debtor, and it was held that "once a mortgage, always a mortgage."

> Justice is due even to the lowest of mankind, and nothing can be lower than the condition and future of a slave. And yet those prescribe wisely who enjoin us to put them upon the same footing as hired laborers, obliging them to do their work, and giving them their dues. Now, as injustice may be done two ways, by force or fraud, fraud being the property of a fox, force that of a lion; both are utterly violative of social duty, but fraud is the more detestable. But in the whole system of villainy, none is more capital than that of the men who, when they most deceive, so manage as that they may seem to be virtuous men.[100]

If Injustice were a Goddess for men to worship, her temples would swarm with votaries, and her statues in bronze be fitly placed in the halls of legislation, in our departments and bureaus of Executive Government, in all the fields of political controversy, in the marts of trade, in the doorways of the conductors of public journals; for it is rare to find justice as the law of conduct and dealing, of action, enactment and decision, of debate and discussion and consideration of motive and character, and weighing of opinion, in any of these places. Men are, above all things else, unjust, uncharitable and intolerant, and in all the affairs of men injustice chiefly rules. The civilized man is less just than the barbarian, and in some respects, free governments are more unjust than the despots.

> Beneficence and liberality are virtues most consistent with a manly nature; but we are always to take care lest our kindnesses should work injury to those whom they are meant to assist, and to others. In the next place, they ought not to exceed our abilities, and they ought to be

---

[100] Cicero, *De Officii* 1.13, in Edmonds (1871), 24–5

bestowed on each in proportion to his deserts. This is the fundamental standard of justice, to which all these things should be referred. For they who do kindnesses which prove of disservice to the person whom they pretend to oblige, are not to be esteemed beneficent or generous, but injurious sycophants. And they who injure one party, in order to be liberal to another, are guilty of the same dishonesty as if they should appropriate to themselves what belongs to another.

Our next part of circumspection is, that our generosity never should exceed our abilities. For they who are more generous then their circumstances admit of are, first, guilty in this, that they wrong their relations; because they bestow upon strangers those means which they might, with greater justice, give or leave to those who are nearest to them. Now a generosity of this kind is generally attended with a lust to ravish and to plunder, in order to be furnished with the means to give away. For it is easy to observe, that most of them are not so much by nature generous, as they are misled by a kind of pride to do a great many things in order that they may seem to be generous; which things seem to spring not so much from good will as from ostentation. Now such a simulation is more nearly allied to duplicity than to generosity or virtue.[101]

3d, OF FORTITUDE.

When the four springs from which virtue and honesty rise are laid open, that which is done with a lofty spirit, and one which scorns ordinary interests, appears the most noble. ... in our praises, we eulogize in a loftier style, actions performed with magnanimity, fortitude and virtue.... But that magnanimity which manifests itself amid toils and dangers, if it be devoid of justice, and contend not for the public good, but for selfish interest, is blameworthy; for, so far from being a mark of virtue, it is

---

[101] Cicero, *De Officii* 1.14, in Edmonds (1871), 26

rather that of a barbarity which is repulsive to all humanity.[102]

Mere animal courage may be possessed by the by the worst of men, and belongs to the sparrow and still smaller creatures. "Fortitude is therefore, rightly defined by the Stoics when they call it, 'valour fighting on the side of justice.'"[103]

But it is the self-same valour, when, changing sides, it fights on the side of injustice. The Swiss have been equally brave, on whatever side they have fought; and heroism has been very generally displayed with little consideration whether the side on which it fought were in the right or in the wrong. Men fight for pay, for their flag, for their king, and above all for glory; and that glory which is won by the victories of an unjust cause is a precious to them as any other.

> No man, therefore, who has acquired the reputation of fortitude, attained his glory by deceit and malice; for nothing that is devoid of justice can be a virtue.
>
> It is, therefore finely said by Plato, that not only the knowledge that is apart from justice, deserves the appellation of cunning, rather than wisdom, but also a soul that is ready to encounter danger, if it be animated by private interest, and not public utility, deserves the character of audaciousness, rather than of fortitude. We hold, therefore, that all men of courage and magnanimity must be at same time men of virtue and single mindedness, lovers of truth and by no means deceitful; for these qualities are the main glory of justice.... They who oppose not, those who commit injustice, are to be deemed brave and courageous.[104]

Glory, among men, is the mead of bravery; and great courage, accomplishing great exploits in war, is deemed to be the chief of all excellencies. Nevertheless, courage or fortitude is not a virtue, nor, in itself, any more admirable or excellent in a man than in an animal. It is possessed by the good and the bad, the worthy and the unworthy, the cruel and the generous, the hireling man-at-arms or freelance and the

---

[102] Cicero, *De Officii* 1.18–19, in Edmonds (1871), 33
[103] Cicero, *De Officii* 1.19, in Edmonds (1871), 33
[104] Cicero, *De Officii* 1.19, in Edmonds (1871), 33–4

noble gentleman and knight alike. Most men worship and glorify it for itself, without reference to that whereof it is the fruit, and which it owes its being. And those who, like Plato and Cicero, esteem it only when its cause and motive are excellent, confound it with these, and esteem it to be itself, and when its cause is pure and virtuous and noble. It is the martyr's faith, the patriot's devotion to his country, the friend's loyalty to his friend, the true woman's love, the generous man's self-sacrificing spirit, that are the excellencies, who strength and purity are shown and proven by the daring and the fortitude which these cause them to display. It is not the bravery of the vessel's captain, who goes calmly with her down into the depths of the sea, or of the engineer who stands firmly at his post until collision shatters his train, or of the leader of the forlorn hope, or of the rescuer of shipwrecked men, that is to be admired and remembered in song and story, but the strong sense of duty in each, overcoming all dread of danger and death. It is the martyr's faith and enthusiasm that makes him brave. It is the wife's love, of which her courage in danger is born. It is the devotion to right, truth and justice that makes true men scorn obloquy and popular condemnation, and bear with fortitude the frowns of prince or people, or the merciless scourgings of evil fortune. The bad may be as brave as the good, the base and brutal as the serenely excellent; but the courage of one is worthless because it proceeds from nothing generous or noble; and that of the other is admirable, not for itself or as a virtue, but as the fruit and flower of the highest and best qualities of manhood.

A spirit altogether heroic and elevated is chiefly discernable by two characteristics. The first consists in a low estimate of mere outward circumstances, since it is convinced that man ought to admire, desire or court nothing but what is virtuous and becoming; and that he ought to succumb to no man, nor to any perturbation either of spirit or fortune. The other is, that, possessed of such a spirit, one should perform actions that are great and of the greatest utility, but extremely arduous, full of difficulties and dangers both to life and the many things that pertain to life.

In the latter of these two consists all the glory, the majesty and the utility; but the causes, and the efficient means that form great men, are in the former, which contains the principles that elevate the soul, and gives it a contempt for temporary considerations. Now, this very excellence consists in two particulars: you are to deem that only to be good, that is virtuous; and you must be free from all mental irregularity. For we are to look upon it as the character of a noble and elevated soul, to slight all those considerations that the generality of mankind account great and glorious, and to despise them, upon firm and durable principles; while strength of mind and greatness of resolution are discerned in bearing these calamities, which, in the cause of human life, are many and various, so as not to be driven from your natural disposition, nor from the dignity of a wise man: for it is not consistent that he who is not subdued by fear, should be subjugated by passion; nor that he who has shown himself not to be overcome by toil, should be conquered by pleasure.[105]

The examples of civil courage are no less meritorious than those of military courage: and they require a greater degree of zeal and labour than these.[106]

Now all that excellence which springs from a lofty and noble nature is altogether produced by the mental, and not by the bodily powers. Meanwhile, the body ought to be kept in such action and order, as that it may be always ready to obey the dictates of reason and wisdom, in carrying them into execution, and in persevering under hardships. But with regard to that honorableness of which we are speaking, it consists wholly in the thoughtful applications of the mind; by which the civilians who preside over public affairs are equally serviceable to their country as they who wage wars.

The character of a brave and resolute man is not to be ruffled with adversity, and not to be in such confusion as to quit his post, as we say, but to preserve a presence of mind, and the exercise of reason, without departing from his purpose. And while this is the characteristic of a lofty spirit, so this also is that of a powerful intellect, namely,

---

[105] Cicero, *De Officii* 1.20, in Edmonds (1871), 35
[106] Cicero, *De Officii* 1.22, in Edmonds (1871), 39–40

to anticipate the future in thought, and to conclude beforehand what may happen on each side, and upon that, what measures to pursue, and never to be surprised so as to say, "I had not thought of that." Such are the operations of a capacious and elevated genius, of such an one as relies on its own prudence and counsel; but to rush precipitately into the field, and to encounter the enemy with mere physical force, has somewhat in it that is barbarous and brutal. But where the occasion and its necessity compel it, we should strenuously resist, and prefer death to slavery or dishonor.[107]

We should never so entirely avoid danger, as to appear irresolute and cowardly; but at the same time, we should avoid unnecessarily exposing ourselves to danger, than which nothing can be more foolish.

The conducting of enterprises is sometimes dangerous to the undertaker, and sometimes to the State, and hence some are in danger of losing their lives, some their reputation, and some their popularity. But we ought to be more forward to expose our own persons than the general interests to danger, and to be more ready to fight for honour and reputation than for other advantages.

Though many have been known cheerfully to venture not only their money but their lives for the public, yet those very men have refused to suffer the smallest loss of glory even at the request of their country.... It was a deadly blow to the Lacedæmonians, when, from a fear of public odium, Cleombrotus fought with Epamonidas, and the power of the Lacedæmonians perished. How preferable was the conduct of Quintus Maximus, of whom Ennius says:

"The man who saved his country by delay,
No tales could move him, and no envy sway;
And thus the laurels on his honored brow,
In age shall flourish, and with time shall grow."

---

[107] Cicero, *De Officii* 1.23, in Edmonds (1871), 41–2

This is a kind of fault which ought also to be avoided in civil matters; for there are some men who, from a dread of unpopularity, dare not express their opinion, however excellent they may be.[108]

4th, OF TEMPERANCE.

Every human action to be free from precipitancy and negligence, nor indeed ought we to do any thing for which we cannot give a justifiable reason. This indeed almost amounts to a definition of duty. Now we must manage so as to keep the appetites subservient to reason that they may neither outstrip it nor fall behind through sloth and cowardice. Let them be always composed and free from all perturbation of spirit; and thus entire consistency and moderation will display themselves....

All the appetites ought to be limited and moderated; all our attention and diligence ought to be awake, so that we do nothing in a rash, random, thoughtless, inconsiderate manner. For nature has not formed this to sport and merryment, but rather to seriousness and studies that are important and sublime. Sport of merriment are not always this allowable; but we are to use them as we do sleep, and other kind of repose, when we have dispatched our weighty and important affairs....

There is likewise a certain limit to be reserved, even in our amusements, that we do not give up every thing to amusement, and that, after being elevated by pleasure, we do not sink into some immorality.[109]

If a man shall have any delight in pleasure, he ought to be extremely observant of his limits in its indulgence. Therefore the nourishment and address of our bodies should be with a view not to our pleasure, but to our health and strength; and should we consider the excellence and dignity of our nature, we should then be made sensible how shameful it is to melt away in pleasure, and to live in voluptuousness and effeminacy;

---

108 Cicero, *De Officii* 1.24, in Edmonds (1871), 43–4
109 Cicero, *De Officii* 1.29, in Edmonds (1871), 52–53

and how noble it is to live with abstinence, with modesty, with strictness and with sobriety.[110]

As we are very properly enjoined, and all the course of our life, to avoid all fits of passion, that is, excess of the emotions of the mind, uncontrolled by reason; in like manner, our conversation ought to be free from all such emotions; so that neither resentment manifest itself, nor undue desire, nor slovenly nest, nor indolence, nor anything of the kind.... Let all passion be avoided; for with that nothing can be right wisely done, nothing with discretion. It is advisable, even in these disputes which take place with our bitterest enemies, if we hear any thing insulting to ourselves, to maintain our equanimity and prepress passion; for whatever is done under such excitement can never be either consistently performed, or approved of by those who are present.[111]

In undertaking every action, we are to regard three things. First, that appetite be subservient to reason, then which there is no condition better fitted for faith, fully performing our moral duties. We are, secondly, to examine how important the object is which we desire to accomplish, that our attention or labor may be neither more or less then the occasion requires. Thirdly, we are to take care that everything that comes under the head of magnificence and dignity shall be well regulated. Now, the best ordering is, the same graceful property be observed which I have recommended.[112]

I am now to speak concerning the order and the timing of things. In this science is comprehended with the Greeks call ευταξια [*eftaxia*, "orderliness"], in which the preservation of order is involved.

Under this head I speak of moderation and Temperance.[113]

---

[110] Cicero, *De Officii* 1.30, in Edmonds (1871), 54
[111] Cicero, *De Officii* 1.38, in Edmonds (1871), 66–67
[112] Cicero, *De Officii* 1.39, in Edmonds (1871), 68
[113] Cicero, *De Officii* 1.40, in Edmonds (1871), 69

As all virtue is a result of four qualities, Prudence, Justice, Magnanimity and Moderation, so the choice of duty, those qualities must necessarily come in completion with one another....

Of all virtues, the most leading is that Wisdom which the Greeks call σοφια [*sophia*], provide that sagacity which they term φρονησις [*phronesis*], we understand quite another thing, as it implies the knowledge of what things are to be desired, and what to be avoided. But that wisdom which I have stated to be the chief, is the knowledge of things divine and human, which comprehends the fellowship of God and men, and their association within themselves. If that be, as it certainly is, the highest of all objects, it follows of course that the duty resulting from this fellowship is the highest of all duties....

The duties of justice are preferable to the studies and duties of knowledge, relating as they do to the interests of the human race, no consideration paramount where to ought to exist in the mind of man.[114]

Men, being associated by nature, manifest their skill in thinking and acting. Therefore, unless knowledge is connected with that virtue which consists in doing service to mankind, that is, in improving human society, it would seem to be but solitary and barren.

In like manner, greatness of soul, one utterly disunited from the company and society of men, becomes a kind of uncouth ferocity. Hence it follows that the company and as a community of men are preferable to mere speculative knowledge. Every duty that operates in the good of human community and society, is preferable to that duty which is united to speculation and knowledge.[115]

But the duties of that society which is most suitable to nature, are not preferable to moderation and decency. Some things are partly so disgraceful and partly so

---

114 Cicero, *De Officii* 1.43, in Edmonds (1871), 73–74
115 Cicero, *De Officii* 1.44, in Edmonds (1871), 75

animal, in their nature, that a wise man could not commit them even to save his country. But unfortunately happens that there never can be a conjuncture, when the public interest shall require from a wise man the performance of such actions....

In the choice of the duties we are to prefer that kind of duty that constitutes to the good of society. In well directed action is always the result of knowledge and prudence. And therefore it is of more consequence to act properly, then to deliberate justly. There are degrees of duties in society, by which every man may understand what is appropriate to himself. The first is owing to the immortal gods, the second to our country, and the third our parents; and lastly to others, through different gradations.[116]

In the third Book *de Officiis*, Cicero says, "of Prudence, which craft is apt to imitate, and likewise of justice, which is always expedient, we have already treated. Two parts of virtue remain, of which the one is discern in the greatness and preeminence of an elevated mind; the other, in the habit and rule continents and Temperance."[117]

It seemed expedient to Ulysses, he says, to wish to escape from the military service, by pretending insanity. It was a dishonorable device. But some may say that it was advantageous to him to rain and live at ease, in Ithaca, with his parents, his wife and his son. "They may ask, do you think any glory arising from daily toils and perils is to be compared with his tranquility? I do verily think that with such tranquility is to be despised or reject; because I think that tranquility which was not honorable, was not even advantageous.[118]

He instances Regulus, who was sent by Hannibal to Rome, bound by an oath that unless certain noble captives should be restored to the Carthaginians, he would himself returned to Carthage; and who, arriving at Rome, might have remained there with his family, retaining his consular rank. Who, he asks, can deny that these things are profitable? "Whom do you think?" he asks, and the answer, "Greatness of mind and Fortitude deny it."[119] "For it is characteristic of these

---

116 Cicero, *De Officii* 1.45, in Edmonds (1871), 76
117 Cicero, *De Officii* 3.25, in Edmonds (1871), 157
118 Cicero, *De Officii* 3.26, in Edmonds (1871), 157
119 Cicero, *De Officii* 3.26, in Edmonds (1871), 158

virtues to fear nothing, to hold all human interests cheap, to think nothing that can happen to a man intolerable."[120] He advised the Senate to detain the captives, and returned to Carthage to die by torture. "At the very time when he was dying he went to sleep, his state and condition were better than they would have been if he had remained at home an aged captive and a perjurer consular.... Can that which is inexpedient for country, expedient for any citizen?"[121]

And he says,

> Men pervert those things that are the foundations of nations, when they separate expediency from virtue. For we all desire our own interest... Who was there that does not most eagerly pursue it? But because we never can find real advantage, except in good report, honor and virtue, therefore we esteem those things first and chief; we consider the name of futility not so much noble and necessary.[122]

> Now, as to what they say, that whatever is very useful becomes virtuous, I say, Nay, it is so really, and does not merely become so; for nothing is expedient which is not likewise virtuous; and it is not because it is expedient that it is virtuous; but because it is virtuous it is expedient....[123]

Most truly Cicero says, though it seemed wonderful to the men of his time that Regulus should have returned, he could not do otherwise, at that time. "Therefore that was not the merit of the man, but of the times. For our ancestors were of opinion that there was no tie closer than an oath, to bind faith."[124]

In the earlier days of republics, men in high stature cannot be otherwise than honest and upright. But the degenerate times come, and much sooner than they did at Rome, when the public sense of right and justice becomes bold and blunted and the morals depraved, contaminated and corrupted; and then it is easy in general for men in public station to prefer expediency will to justice, and profit to honesty

---

[120] Cicero, *De Officii* 3.27, in Edmonds (1871), 158
[121] Cicero, *De Officii* 3.27, in Edmonds (1871), 158
[122] Cicero, *De Officii* 3.28, in Edmonds (1871), 159
[123] Cicero, *De Officii* 3.30, in Edmonds (1871), 164
[124] Cicero, *De Officii* 3.30, in Edmonds (1871), 164

and honor. Then Liberty exists only by precarious title; legislators sell their votes and judges their decisions, public offices are public robbers, course vulgarity and neighborly are enthroned side-by-side; and everything is unclean, impure and feculent.

Virtue, in the Roman sense of the word, was man himself, from the word *vir*, a man, *honestas* was more than honesty. The old English word "the grand name" of "gentlemen" expresses a character containing both: for *honestas* was honor, gentility, courtesy, high breeding and decorum.

A people so debauched and with the moral sense so diseased as not to be ashamed of the baseness and venality of those whom it has made its chiefs, in whose estimation falsehood no longer dishonors those set in high places and whom venal legislation and an organized system of public plunder do not stir to indignation and wrath, are emasculated of their virtue also, and care little when the country is humiliated by indignities offered it by other States. And it is plain, Cicero tells us, "that those acts which are done with a timid, humble timid abject and broken spirit, are inexpedient, because they are scandalous, foul and base."[125]

> The fourth part [of virtue] is comprehended in propriety, moderation, modesty, continence and temperance. Can any thing, [he asks,] be expedient which is contrary to this train of such virtues?" The Cyrenæans ... have made all good consistent pleasure ... and Epicurus is the advocate and author of the same opinion. Against these we must fight, with man and horse, as it is said, if we need to defend and hold fast to virtue. ... For where will there be room for Prudence? ... How miserable the servitude of virtue, when it is the slave of pleasure? Moreover, what would be the office of Prudence? To select pleasures ingeniously? Admit that nothing could be more delightful than this; what can be imagined more base? What room can Fortitude, which is the condemning of pain and toil, have in his system who calls pain the greatest of evils? ... How can he commend temperance, who makes the chief good to consistent pleasure? For temperance is hostile to irregular passions; but irregular passions are the companions of pleasure. ... Justice staggers, or rather falls to the ground, and calls those

---

[125] Cicero, *De Officii* 3.32, in Edmonds (1871), 166

virtues which are discerned in society, and the association of mankind. For neither kindness, nor liberality, nor courtesy can exist, any more than friendship, if they are not sought for their own sakes, but are referred to pleasure and interest. … As there is no expediency which can be contrary to virtue; so all bodily pleasure is opposed to virtue."[126]

When that which seems useful in friendship is compared with that which is virtuous, let the appearance of expediency be disregarded, let virtue prevail. Moreover, when in friendship, things are not virtuous shall be required of us, obligation and good faith should be preferred to friendship.[127]

It is in state affairs that men most frequently commit crimes under the pretext of expediency. But nothing that is cruel can be expedient. Those are noble actions, in which the appearance of public expediency is treated with contempt in comparison with virtue. So great is the power of virtue, that it throws the seeming of expediency into the shade.[128]

What is base never is expedient, not even when you obtain by it what you think to be useful….[129]

If the Aquilian definition is true, pretense and dissimulation ought to be banished from the whole of life; so that the good man will not pretend or conceal anything, to the end of buying or selling with profit…. Criminal devices embodied in pretense, wherefore all deceit should be excluded from contracts. To him who disavows that he would do, for the sake of his own gain, only so much as is not illegal, neither great pains nor thanks are due…. To do wrong is never really profitable,

---

[126] Cicero, *De Officii* 3.33, in Edmonds (1871), 166–67
[127] Cicero, *De Officii* 3.10, in Edmonds (1871), 132
[128] Cicero, *De Officii* 3.11, in Edmonds (1871), 132–33
[129] Cicero, *De Officii* 3.12, in Edmonds (1871), 134

because it is always base; and to be a good man is always profitable, because it is always virtuous.[130]

> We need not dread Jove, lest in his anger he should do us harm, who neither is accustomed to be angry nor to do harm. In our oath it ought to be considered, not what is the fear, but what is force…. In an oath is a religious affirmation; but what you solemnly promise, as if God were witness, to that you ought to adhere…. In it does not, when sworn, pertain to the anger of the gods, there be no such thing, but to justice and fidelity…. He who violates an oath, violates faith, which are ancestors placed in the capitol, its statue next to that of Jupiter Optimus Maximus."[131]

The oath is faith-pledged in truth, promised to men, unto God, and more sacred than the common promise, express or implied, only because God is invoked to punish its violation. The obligation to keep it is no greater than the obligation to keep any other promise: for the degree of penalty or punishment for violation of promise, vow or obligation, in no wise or degree increases the weight of the obligation or makes it more stringent, nor the punishment to be greater; since one who promises or vows cannot himself fix the punishment, as one can for a pecuniary penalty. God's measure of crime and punishment may be very different from ours.

The fifth paradox of Cicero is, "The wise man alone is free, and that every fool is a slave." And in his commentary upon it he says,

> Let a general be celebrated, or let him be honored with that title, or let him be thought worthy of it. But how, or over what freeman will he exercise control, who cannot command his own passions? They came, in the first place, bridled his lusts, let him despise pleasures, let him subdue anger, they can get the better of avarice, let him expunge the other stains in his character, and then, when he himself is no longer in subjection to disgrace and degradation, the most savage tyrants let him than, I say, begin to others. But while he is subservient to these,

---

130 Cicero, *De Officii* 3.15, in Edmonds (1871), 138–39
131 Cicero, *De Officii* 3.29, in Edmonds (1871), 159–60

> not only is he not to be regarded as a general, but he is by
> no means to be considered as even a free man.[132]

Sir Thomas Browne says, "Rest not in an ovation, but a triumph over thy passions. Let anchor walk pain down the head, let malice go manacled, and in the fettered, after the. Behold within thee the long train by trophies, not without thee. Chain up the unruly Legion of life breast. Lead thine own captivity captive, and be Cæsar are within thyself."[133]

> To chase our enemies out of the field, and be led captive your vices; to beat down our foes, and fall down to our concupiscences; are solecisms in moral schools, and no laurel attends thereon.... Weapons for such confidence are not to be forged at Lipara; Vulcan's art does nothing in this internal militia; wherein not the armor of Achilles, but the armature of St. Paul, gives the glorious day, and triumphs, not leading up into capitols, but up into the highest heavens. And, therefore, while so many think it the only valor to command and master others, study thou the dominion of thyself, and quiet thine own commotions. Let right reason be thy Lycurgus, and lift up thy hand unto the law of it; move by thy intelligences of the superior faculties, not by the rapt of passion, nor merely by that of temper and constitution. They who are merely carried on by the wheel of such inclinations, without the hand and guidance of sovereign reason, are but the automatous part of mankind, rather lived than living, or at least underliving themselves.[134]

Cicero, *Upon the Duties of a Magistrate*, addressed to his brother Quintus Cicero, proprætor of Asia Minor, says, "It is a glorious thing for a man to have been invested with the three years sovereign power in Asia, in such a manner that no statue, no picture, no plate, no government, no slave, no beauty, no hoard of money, in which things

---

132 Cicero, *Paradoxes*, 5, in Edmonds (1871), 277-78
133 Thomas Browne, *Christian Morals* (Cambridge University Press, 1716), 1.2
134 Browne, *Christian Morals* (1716), 1.24

this province abounds, ever caused him to swerve from his countenance and moderation."[135]

And in his *Oration for the Manilian Law*, eulogizing the continence of Pompey in Asia Minor, he said, "Neither did avarice call him away from the course he had laid down, to the acquisition of any gain, nor his passions to any pleasure, nor the magnificence of a city to acquaint himself with it, nor fatigue itself to repose."[136] In the same letter to his brother he says,

> In human nature at large, and especially at our time of life, it is very difficult for a man to alter his disposition, or suddenly to pluck out a failing that has settled into a habit. But my advice to you is this, if you can not altogether avoid this, but passion takes possession of your mind before reason can take precautions that it should not invade it, you should undergo a course of preparation, and be every day meditating that resistance must be offered to anger, and the more violently it affects the mind, the more diligently must you restrain your tongue.[137]

"Cultivate justice and piety; which, while it should be great," Cicero says in his *Vision of Scipio*, "toward your parents and relations, should be greatest toward your country. Such a life is the path to heaven."[138] And |William| Godwin says, |*Enquiry Concerning*| *Political Justice*, Book 5, Chap. 16,

> A wise and well-informed man will not fail to be the votary of liberty and justice. He will be ready to exert himself in their defense wherever they exist. It can not be a matter of indifference to him when his own liberty and that of other men, with whose merits and capacities he has the best opportunity of being acquainted, are involved in the event of the struggle to be made; but his attachment will be to the cause, as the cause of man and not to the country. Wherever there are individuals who

---

135 Cicero, *Duties of a Magistrate*, in Edmonds (1871), 309
136 Cicero, *Pro Lege Manilia*, in Edmonds (1871), 309
137 Cicero, *Duties of a Magistrate*, in Edmonds (1871), 325
138 Cicero, *The Vision of Scipio*, in Edmonds (1871), 293

understand the value of political justice, and are prepared to assert it, that is his country; wherever he can most contribute to the diffusion of these principles, and the real happiness of mankind, that is his country. Nor does he desire for any country, any other benefit than justice.[139]

"The rule as to profit," Cicero says, "is the same as that which obtains respecting honesty. To him who will not thoroughly perceive this, no fraud, no villainy will be wanting; for, considering thus, 'that, indeed, is honest, but this is expedient,' he will dare erroneously to separate things united by nature—which is the fountain of all frauds, malpractices, and crimes."[140]

The just man, and he whom we deem a good man, would take nothing from any man in order to transfer it wrongfully to himself... Nothing is either expedient or useful which is unjust. He who has not learned this, can not be a good man.... Nothing is expedient which is not morally right, even though you could obtain it without any body proving you guilty....

What is there which that expediency, as it is called, can bring, so valuable as that which it takes away, if it deprive you of the name of a good man, if it rob you of your integrity and justice? Now, what difference does it make, whether from a man one transform himself into a beast, or under the form of a man, bear the savage nature of a beast?[141]

Expediency then, should be guided by virtue, and indeed so that these two may seem to differ from each other in name, but to signify the same in reality. In vulgar opinion I know not what advantage can be greater than that of sovereign sway, but, on the contrary, when I begin to recall my reason to the truth, I find nothing more disadvantageous to him who shall have attained it unjustly.... If these things be not profitable, which seem so in the highest degree, because they are full of disgrace

---

139 Quoted in Edmonds (1871), 293
140 Cicero, *De Officii* 3.18, Edmonds (1871), 145
141 Cicero, *De Officii* 3.20, Edmonds (1871), 148

and turpitude, we ought to be quite convinced that there is nothing expedient which is not virtuous.[142]

Amid the alterations of prosperous and adverse fortunes of parties in any Republic, anyone whose memory is not wholly unserviceable may remember many things done by a party once in party, and which has now lost the direction of affairs, which in later days, imitated by their conquerors, have returned as evil precedents, to plague and punish their inventors. They seemed expedient, at the time, though unjust, and profitable, though rascally and navish; and so they were used, and the profit of them reaped; and a heavy debt incurred, now being paid to men with usurious and compounded interest.

Such, for a single example, has been the custom, commenced 40 years or more ago, the Congress of the United States, of deciding cases of contested election, not as a court of justice decides, upon the law and the facts, and according to right and justice (although in every such case the house deciding is, for that matter and occasion, a court of justice, acting judiciously, under all the solemn obligations of judges), but, more simply, in favor of the party who belonged to the dominant faction. Every such case was a great wrong to the person unjustly denied his seat, and a greater wrong to the people and constituency who had elected him; and it also involved willful and deliberate perjuring: and yet very rarely was such a contest decided upon any other ground. Another party, coming into power afterwards, adopted the evil habit, using without scruples of conscience the same weapons of offense; and thus, surely though late, the punishment results from the offense and wrong, as a consequence from cause. Every injustice is prolific and bears its fruit in due season. *Historiæ decus est, et quasi anima, ut cum eventis causce copulentur,*[143] "It is the beauty and, as it were, the soul, of history, that events are duly connected with their causes."

All the victories that expediency wins over justice; are Cadmæun conquests, in which the victor suffers more than he does was thus overcome. "For God beholds thee," Menander says, "being near at hand, who is pleased with just deeds, and not with unjust."[144] *'Opsé Theōn 'aléonsi múloi, 'aléonsi dè letptá |Οψε θεών αλέουσι μύλοι, αλέουσι δε*

---

[142] Cicero, *De Officii* 3.20, Edmonds (1871), 150–51

[143] Francis Bacon, *De Augmentis Scientiaurum* [On the Advancement of Learning] (Argentorati [Strassburg]: Johan. Joachimi Bockenhoferi, 1654), Liber 2, Cap. 4 [p. 91]

[144] H.T. Riley, *Dictionary of Latin Quotations, Proverbs, Maxims, and Mottos, Classical and Mediaeval: Including Law Terms and Phrases. With a Selection of Greek Quotations* (London: Bell & Daldy, 1866), 542

λεπτά|, the Greek proverb said, "the mills of the Gods grind late, but they grind fine."[145]

It is as true now, as it was when Cicero wrote the sentence, that in guilt there cannot be glory; and that, "if power is to be sought by any means whatever, it cannot be expedient, when allied to infamy."[146] The product of bad seed is always worthy of it, and justice as unerringly punishes nations in the end, as it does the individual. There is no remission of sins for nations. And if one reserves to itself, by its constitution of government, the power to violate the obligations of its contracts, and by near law to annul its own solemn promises; if it refuses remedy of justice to those who have rightful demands against itself, the seeds so sown must in the end bear its evil and disastrous fruit of consequences. "Odium and infamy cannot be useful to any Empire which ought to be supported by glory and the goodwill of its allies...."[147]

"It is great valor," he said,

> ...if one elevated to the magistracy, in a kingdom were virtue hath consideration, changes not his morals, how great soever the honors be to which he is advanced; if you there preserves all the good habit which he had one only private man; if you permit not himself to be led away with pride and vanity. If, in the kingdom were virtue and laws are condemned, in the confusion and disorder which there prevail, he himself is depressed with poverty, afflicted, reduced even to the loss of life, but yet, in the midst of so many miseries, he remains constant, preserves all the innocence he of his manners, and never changes his opinion; Ah! How great and illustrious is this valor![148]

---

[145]*Oracula Sybillina* 8.14

[146] Cicero, *De Officii* 3.22, Edmonds (1871), 151

[147] Cicero, *De Officii* 3.22, Edmonds (1871), 152

[148] Pike ascribes this remark to Cicero, although it is otherwise ascribed to Confucius. While transcribing, Pike had two books opened, and made his misattribution. The quote appears in [Anon.], *The Phenix: a Collection of Old and Rare Fragments: viz. The Morals of Confucius, the Chinese Philosopher; the Oracles of Zoroaster, the Founder of the Religion of the Persian Magi; Sanchoniatho's History of the Creation; The Voyages of Hanno Round the Coast of Africa, Five Hundred Years Before Christ; King Hiempsal's History of the African Settlements, Translated from the Punic Books; and the Choice Sayings of Publius Syrus* (New York: William Gowan, 1835), 67.

"The perfect man," Cu-su[149] said,

> ...governs himself according to his present state, and covets nothing beyond it. If he find himself in the midst of riches, he acts like a rich man, but addicts not himself to unlawful pleasure; he avoids luxury, detests pride, offends nobody. If he is in a poor and contemptible state, he acts as a poor and mean man ought to act; but he does nothing unworthy of a grave and worthy man. If he be remote from his own country, he behaves himself as a stranger ought to do; but he is always like himself. If he is in affliction and adversity, he does not insolently affront his destiny, but has courage and resolution; nothing can shake his constancy. If he is advanced to the dignities of state, he keeps his rank, but never treats his inferiors with severity; and if he sees himself below others, he is humble; he never departs from the respect he owes to his superiors; he never purchases their favor with flattery. He uses his utmost endeavors to perfect himself, and exacts nothing of others with severity. It is upon this account that he expresses no discontent or anger to any person. If he lift up his eyes towards heaven, it is not to complain because it has not sent him prosperity, or to murmur because it afflicts him. If he looks down towards the ground, it is not to reproach men, and attribute the cause of his miseries and necessities unto them; it is to testify his humility; that is to say, that he is always contented with his condition, that he desires nothing beyond it, and that, with submission and an even spirit, he expects whatever heaven shall ordain concerning him. Thus he rejoiceth in a certain tranquility, which may well be compared to the top of those mountains which are higher than the region where the thunder and tempests are formed.[150]

This is a maxim ascribed to Zarathustra: "Foresee misfortunes, that thou mayest strive to prevent them; but, whenever they happen, bear

---

[149] "Cu-su" was a fictionalized Chinese philosopher appearing in 18th-century European literature. He first appeared in a "Chinese catechism" in Voltaire's anonymous *Dictionnaire philosophique, portatif* (Londres [false imprint; i.e., Geneva], 1764), 91

[150] [Anon.], *The Phenix* (1835), 70–1

them with magnanimity. It is the very height of calamity, not to be able to support it."[151]

The laws of justice was summed up by the disciple Confucius in this one sentence: "Do to another what you would he should do unto you: and do not to another what you would not should be done unto you."[152] And if we always judged others and their motives, as we wish our conduct and motives to be judged, we should be both juster and wiser than we are.

"Above all things," Cicero says,

> ...to be content with what we possess, is the greatest and most secure of riches. If therefore they who are the most skillful valuers of property highly estimate fields in certain sites, because such estates are the least liable to injury, how much more valuable is virtue, which never can be wrested never can be filched from us, which cannot be lost by fire or by shipwreck, and which is not alienated by the convulsions of tempest or of time, with which those who are endowed alone are rich, for they alone possess resources which are profitable and eternal; and they are the only men who, being contented with what they possess, think it sufficient, which is the criterion of riches: they hanker after nothing, they are in need of nothing, they feel the want of nothing, and they require nothing. As to the unsatiable and avaricious part of mankind, as they have possessions liable to uncertainty, and at the mercy of chance, they who are forever thirsting after more, and of whom there never was a man for whom what he had sufficed; they are so far from being wealthy and rich, that they are to be regarded as necessitous and beggared.[153]

This was a maxim of Confucius, "Always behave yourself with the same caution and discretion as you would do if you were observed by ten eyes, and pointed at by his many hands."[154]

---

151 [Anon.], *The Phenix* (1835), 175

152 [Anon.], *The Phenix* (1835), 58

153 Cicero, *Paradoxes*, 6, in Edmonds (1871), 287

154 Josephus Tela, ed., *The Life and Morals of Confucius, a Chinese Philosopher, who Flourished about Five Hundred Years Before the Coming of Jesus Christ. Being one of the Choisest Pieces of Learning and Morality Remaining of that Nation. Reprinted from the Edition of 1691* [...] (London:

And Cu-su, his disciple, said, "Take heed how you should act when you are alone. Although you should be retired into the most solitary and most private part of your house, you want to do nothing were of you would be ashamed if you were in company or in public."[155]
"Have you desire," he continues,

> ...that I should show you after what manner he that has acquired some perfection governs himself? He keeps a continual watch upon himself; he undertakes nothing, begins nothing, pronounces no word, in which he has not meditated. Before he raises any notion in his heart, he carefully observes himself, he reflects on everything, he examines everything, he is in a continual vigilance. Before he speaks, he is satisfied that what he is about to utter is true and rational; and he thinks that he cannot reap a more pleasant fruit from his vigilance and examination, then to accustom himself circumspectly and wisely to govern himself in the things which are neither seen nor known by any.[156]

Being asked in what valor consisted, and what it was necessary to do to obtain the name of valiant, the Chinese philosopher replied that the valor of his disciples, who applied themselves to the study of wisdom, was, "to act mildly in the education of children and disciple; to be indulgent to them; patiently to bear their disobedience is an defect; by which valor they conquered their violent temper, and submitted their passions, generally violent, to Reason."[157] He said,

> A perfect man (for, in short, the perfect man only can have a true valor), ought always to be busied in conquering himself. He must suit himself to the manners and tempers of others, but he ought always to be master of his own heart and actions. He must not suffer himself to be corrupted by the conversation or examples of loose and effeminate persons. He must never obey, till he has first examined what is commanded him. He must never

---

Printed for the Proprietor, by J. Gillet, Fleet Street. Published by J. Souter, 73, St. Paul's Church-Yard, 1818), 49
[155] Tela, ed., *Life and Morals of Confucius* (1818), 78
[156] Tela, ed., *Life and Morals of Confucius* (1818), 78–9
[157] Tela, ed., *Life and Morals of Confucius* (1818), 66–7

imitate others without judgment. In the midst of so many mad and blind persons, which go at random, he must walk aright, and not incline to any party: this is the true valor.[158]

Even to win the best among what are deemed the prizes of life, such as deserved honor, the good opinion of man, legitimate influence, wealth honestly earned, place and station of which one need not be ashamed, the virtues of a wise prudence, manly fortitude or moral courage, temperance and moderation of self-command, and above all justice, are the most certain and effective instruments and means.

And even these prizes are found, as the end of life draws near, to have been of far less worth in the possession, than they seemed to be when they were striven for or won. Compared with content, and peace of mind, serenity of soul and self-respect, they are hardly worth remembering.

"To my mind," Cicero says,

> ...nothing whatever seems of long duration, in which there is any end. For when that arrives, then the time which has passed has flowed away; that only remains which you have secured by virtue and right conduct. Hours indeed depart from us, and days and months and years; nor does past time ever return, nor can it be discovered what is to follow. Whatever time is assigned to each to live, with that he ought to be content: for neither need the drama be performed entire by the actor, in order to give satisfaction, provided he be approved in whatever act he may be: nor need the wise man live till the *plaudite*.[159] For the short period of life is long enough for living well and honorably; and if you should advance further, you need no more grieve than farmers do, when the loveliness of spring-time hath passed, that summer and autumn have come.[160]

---

[158] Tela, ed., *Life and Morals of Confucius* (1818), 67–8

[159] *Plaudite*, "The last word of the lay which invites applause of the audience. It is here equivalent to the phrase 'the fall of the curtain.'" —Edmonds (1871), 248, fnt. 2

[160] Cicero, *On Old Age*, 29, in Edmonds (1871), 248

The doctrine of the Stoics in regard to the virtues, is thus stated by Diogenes of Laërtia in Cilicia:

> Among the virtues some are primitive and some are derived. The primitive ones are prudence, manly courage, justice, and temperance. And subordinate to these, as a kind of species contained in them, are magnanimity, continence, endurance, presence of mind, wisdom in council. And the Stoics define prudence as a knowledge of what is good, and bad, and indifferent; justice as a knowledge of what ought to be chosen, what ought to be avoided, and what is indifferent; magnanimity as a knowledge of engendering a lofty habit, superior to all such accidents as happen to all men indifferently, whether they be good or bad; continence they consider a disposition which never abandons right reason, or a habit which never yields to pleasure; endurance they call a knowledge or habit by which we understand what we ought to endure, what we ought not, and what is indifferent; presence of mind they define as a habit which is prompt at finding out what is suitable on a sudden emergency; and wisdom in counsel they think a knowledge which leads us to judge what we are to do, and how we are to do it, in order to act becomingly. And analogously, of vices too there are some which are primary, and some which are subordinate; as, for instance, folly, and cowardice, and injustice, and intemperance, are among the primary vices; incontinence, slowness, and folly in counsel among the subordinate ones. And the vices are ignorance of those things of which the virtues are the knowledge.[161]

PRUDENCE.

> He that observes not the alterations of the times, shall seldom be victorious but by chance: but he that cannot alter his course according to the alterations of the times

---

[161] Diogenes Laërtius, *Zeno*, 54, in C. D. Longe, trans., *The Lives and Opinions of Eminent Philosophers by Diogenes Laërtius* (London: Henry G. Bohn, 1853), 293

shall never be a conqueror. He is a wise commander and only he, that can discover the change of times, and changes his proceedings according to the times.[162]

On all designes which require not sudden execution, take mature deliberation, and weigh the convenients, with the inconvenients, and then resolve; after which, neither delay the execution, nor bewray thy intention. He that deceives himself, till he hath made himself master of his desires, layes himself open to his own ruine, and makes himself prisoner of his own tongue.[163]

Carry a watchful eye upon dangers before they come to ripenesse; and when they are ripe, let loose a speedy hand: he that expects them too long, or meets them too soon, gives advantage to the evill: Commit their beginnings to Argus – hundred eyes, and their ends to Briareus – hundred hands, and thou art safe.[164]

It is great prudence to discover an inconvenience in the birth; which, so discovered, is easie to be supprest: but if it ripen into a custom, the sudden remedy thereof is often worse than the disease: in such a case, it is better to temporize a little, than to struggle too much. He that opposes a full-aged inconvenience too suddenly strengthens it.[165]

Give not thy tongue too great a liberty, lest it take thee prisoner. A word unspoken is, like the sword in thy scabbard, thine; if vented, thy sword is in another's hand: if thou desire to be held wise, be so wise as to hold thy tongue.[166]

Be not instable in thy resolutions, nor various in thy actions, nor inconsistent in thy affections. So deliberate, that thou mayst resolve; so resolve, that thou mayst

---

[162] Quarles, *Enchiridion* (1641) 1.8
[163] Quarles, *Enchiridion* (1641) 1.16
[164] Quarles, *Enchiridion* (1641) 1.31
[165] Quarles, *Enchiridion* (1641) 1.35
[166] Quarles, *Enchiridion* (1641) 1.32

perform; so perform that thou mayst persevere: mutability is the badge of infirmity.[167]

In thy discourse take heed what thou speakest, to whom thou speakest, how thou speakest, and when thou speakest: What thou speakest, speak truly; when thou speakest, speak wiselie – A fool's heart is in his tongue; but a wise man's tongue is in his heart.[168]

FORTITUDE

If though desire to be truly valiant, feare to doe any Injury: Hee that fears not to doe evill, is always afraid to suffer evill: Hee that never fears, is desperate: And he that feares always is a Coward: He is the true valiant man, that dares nothing but what he may, and feares nothing but what he ought.[169]

Let every Souldier arme his mind with hopes, and put on courage: Whatsoever dysaster falls, let not his heart sinke. The Passage of providence lyes through many crooked ways; A despairing heart is the true prophet of approaching evill: his Actions may weave the webbes of fortune, but not breake them.[170]

Let the feare of a danger be a spurre to prevent it: Hee that feares otherwise, gives advantage to the danger: It is lesse folly not to endeavor the prevention of the evil thou fearest, then to fear the evill which they endeavor cannot prevent.[171]

Feare nothing, but what thy industry may prevent: Be confidant of nothing but what Fortune can not defeat: it is no lesse Folly to feare what is impossible to be avoided,

---

[167] Quarles, *Enchiridion* (1641) 1.35
[168] Quarles, *Enchiridion* (1641) 3.55
[169] Quarles, *Enchiridion* (1641) 2.59
[170] Quarles, *Enchiridion* (1641) 1.43
[171] Quarles, *Enchiridion* (1641) 4.15

then to be secure when there is a possibility to be depriv'd.[172]

If God hath sent thee a Crosse, take it up and follow Him: use it wisely, lest it be unprofitable; bear it patiently, lest it be intolerable; behold in it God's Anger against sinne, and his Love towards thee; in punishing the one & chastening the other: If it be light, slight it not; if heavy, murmure not: Not to be sensible of a Judgment is the Symptome of a hardened heart; and to bee displeas'd at his Pleasure, is a sign of a rebellious Will.

If thou desire to be magnanimous, undertake nothing rashly, and feare nothing thou undertak'st: Feare nothing but Infamy: Dare anything but Injury: the measure of Magnanimity, is neither to be Rash nor Timorous.

Practice in health to bear sickness, and endeavor in the strength of thy life to entertain death: He that hath a will to die, not having power to live, shewes necessity, not Vertue: It is the glory of a brave mind to embrace pangs in the very arms of pleasure; What name of Vertue merits he, that goes when hee is driven?[173]

TEMPERANCE

Endeavour to subdue as well thy irascible, as thy concupiscible[174] affections: To endure injuries with a brave minde, is one halfe of the conquest; and to abstain from pleasing evils with a courageous spirit is the other: The summe of all humanity, and height of moral perfection, is bear and forbear.[175]

Let not thy fancy be guided by thine eye; nor let thy will be governed by thy fancy: Thine eye may be deceived in her object, and thy fancy may be deluded in her subject: let thy understanding moderate between thine

---

172 Quarles, *Enchiridion* (1641) 4.38
173 Quarles, *Enchiridion* (1641) 4.41–43
174 *Irascible*, "easily-angered'; *concuspiscible*, "lustful or covetous."
175 Quarles, *Enchiridion* (1641) 2.16

eye and thy fancy; and let thy judgment arbitrate between thy fancy and thy will, so shall thy fancy apprehend what is true: so shall thy will elect what is good.[176]

The way to subject all things to thy selfe, is to subject thy selfe to Reason: Thou shalt govern many, if Reason govern thee: Wouldst thou be crowned the monarch of a little world? Command thy selfe.[177]

So use Prosperity, that Adversity may not abuse thee: if in the one Security admits no fearse, in the other, Despaire will afford no hopes: He that in Prosperity can foretell a danger, can in Adversity foresee deliverance.[178]

Be not too greedy in desiring Riches, nor too eager in seeking them: nor too covetous in keeping them; nor too passionate in losing them: the first will possess thy soul of discontent; the second will dispossesse thy body of Rest; the third will possesse thy wealth of thee; The last will dispossessc thee of thy self: Hee that is too violent in the concupiscible, will be as violent in the irascible.[179]

Wee are borne with our temptations: Nature sometimes presses us to evill, sometimes provokes us unto good; If therefore thou givest her more than her due, thou nourishest an enemy; If less than is sufficient, thou destroyest a friend: Moderation will prevent both.
If thou scorne not to Luxury in thy Youth, Chastity will scorne thy service in thy Age; and that the Will of thy green years thought no Vice in the acting, the necessity of thy gray haires makes no Vertue in the forbearing: Where there is no Conflict, there can be no Conquest; where there is no Conquest, there is no Crowne.[180]

[176] Quarles, *Enchiridion* (1641) 2.15
[177] Quarles, *Enchiridion* (1641) 2.19
[178] Quarles, *Enchiridion* (1641) 2.57
[179] Quarles, *Enchiridion* (1641) 2.64
[180] Quarles, *Enchiridion* (1641) 2.73–74

Make thy Recreations Servants to thy businesses, lest thou become slave to thy Recreations: When thou goest up into the Mountain, leave this servant in the Valley; When thou goest to the city, leave him in the Suburbs. And Remember, The ervant must not be greater than his Master.[181]

So behave thyself in thy course of life as at a banquet. Take what is offer'd with modest thankfulness: and expect what is not as yet offer'd with hopeful patience: let not thy rude Appetite press thee, nor a slight carefulnesse indispose thee, nor a sullen discontent deject thee; Who desires more than enough, hath too much: And he that is satisfied with a little, hath no lesse than enough: |*Bene est cui Deus obtulit parcâ, quod satis est, manu.*|[182]

Hath any wounded thee with injuries? Meet them with patience; hasty words rankle the wound, soft language dresses it, forgivenesse cures it, and oblivion takes away the scar. It is more noble, by silence, to avoid an injury, than by argument to overcome it.[183]

Beware of drunkenness, lest all good men beware of thee; where drunkenness reigns, there reason is an exile, virtue, a stranger; God, an enemy, blasphemy is wit, oaths are rhetoric, and secrets are proclamations. Noah discovered that in one hour drunk, which sober, he kept secret six hundred years.[184]

Temperate men have their passions so balanced within them, that they have none in their height and purity. Though they seldom fall into foul acts, they very rarely shed a luster on their conduct by the excelling

---

[181] Quarles, *Enchiridion* (1641) 4.49

[182] Quarles, *Enchiridion* (1641) 4.70. Pike omits Quarles's partial citation of Horace, *Carmina*, 3.16.42, "Multa pententibus Desunt multa; bene est cui Deus obtulit parcâ quod satis est manu" (Those who desire much are always in need; well for him to whom God gives what is sufficient with a sparing hand).

[183] Quarles, *Enchiridion* (1641) 3.34

[184] Quarles, *Enchiridion* (1641) 3.14

deeds of nobleness. I observe, that in general, the most illustrious heroes have possessed both courage and compassion; and have often had wet eyes as well as wounding hands. I would not rob temperance of her royalty. Fabius may conquer by delaying,[185] as well as Cæsar by expedition. As the world is, temperance is a virtue of singular worth; but without doubt, high spirits directed right, will bear away the palm of more glorious actions. These are best to raise commonwealths; but the other, are best to rule them after.[186]

JUSTICE

If thou hast wronged thy brother in thought, reconcile thee to him in thought. If thou hast offended him in words, let thy reconciliation be in words. If thou hast trespassed against him in deeds, by deeds be reconciled to him. That reconciliation is most kindly, which is most in kind.[187]

Be not censorious, for thou knowest not whom thou judgest. It is a more dexterous error to speak well of an evil man, than ill of a good man, and safer for thy judgment to be misled by simple charity, than uncharitable wisdom; he may tax others with a privilege, that hath not in himself what others may tax.[188]

Let that Commonwealth which de sires to flourish, be very strict, both in her punishments and Rewards, according to the merits of the Subject, and offence of the Delinquent: Let the Service of the Deserver be rewarded, lest thou discourage worth; and let the Crime of the offender be punish'd lest thou encourage Vice: the

---

[185] Quintus Fabius Maximus Verrucosus (died 203 BC) was a Roman general and statesman. Following Hannibal's victory over the Roman army at Cannae, Fabius used caution and delay to wear down the Carthaginians. Thereafter he was called Fabius Cunctator, meaning "Fabius, the delayer."

[186] Owen Felltham, *Resolves, Divine, Moral, and Political* (1677 ed.), 1.45

[187] Quarles, *Enchiridion* (1641) 2.69

[188] Quarles, *Enchiridion* (1641) 3.81

neglect of |the one weakens a commonwealth, the omission of both ruins it|.[189]

In every Relative Action, change Conditions with thy brother; then aske thy Conscience what thou would be done to; Being truly resolved, exchange again, and do thou the like to him, and thy Charity shall never erre: It is injustice to doe, what without impatience thou canst not suffer.[190]

Detain not the wages from the poor man that hath earned it, lest God withhold thy wages from thee: If he complain to thee, hear him, lest he complain to heaven, where he will be heard: If he hunger for thy sake, thou shalt not prosper for his sake. The poor man's penny is a plague in the rich man's purse.[191]

If thou desire Rest unto thy Soule, bee Just. He that doth no injury, fears not to suffer injury: The unjust mind is always in labour: It either practises the evill it hath projected, or Projects to avoid the evill it hath deserved.[192]

What thou hast taken unlawfully, restore speedily, for the sin in taking it, is repeated every minute thou keepest it: if thou canst, restore it in kind; if not, in value: If it may be, restore it to the party; if not, to God: The Poor is God's receiver.[193]

If thou be angry with him that reproves thy Sin, thou secretly confessest his reproof to be just: If thou acknowledge his reproof to be just, thou secretly confessest thy anger to be unjust. He that is angry with the just reprover, kindles the fire of the just Revenger.[194]

---

[189] Quarles, Enchiridion (1641) 1.14. Pike omits the portion between the pipes.
[190] Quarles, *Enchiridion* (1641) 3.45
[191] Quarles, *Enchiridion* (1641) 3.70
[192] Quarles, *Enchiridion* (1641) 3.74
[193] Quarles, *Enchiridion* (1641) 4.14
[194] Quarles, *Enchiridion* (1641) 3.42

If thou stand guilty of oppression, or wrongfully possessed of another's right, see thou make restitution before thou givest an alms; if otherwise, what art thou but a thief, and makest God thy receiver?[195]

If thou wouldest be justified, acknowledge thy injustice. He that confesses his sin, begins his journey towards salvation; he that is sorry for it mends his pace; he that forsakes it, is at his journey's end.

Before thou reprehend another, take heed thou art not culpable in what thou goest about to reprehend. He that cleanses a blot with blotted fingers, makes a greater blur.[196]

What thou givest to the poor, thou securest from the thief; but what thou withholdest from his necessity, a thief possesses. God's exchequer is the poor man's box: when thou strikest a tally he becomes thy debtor.[197]

When Solon was asked how men could be most effectually deterred from committing injustice, he said, "If those who are not injured feel as much indignation as those who are.[198]

And it is true that things will not long go well in a State when acts of injustice and wrongs do not arouse the righteous indignation of those who do not themselves suffer injury from them. When the rights of his citizen can be wantonly invaded by any branch of the government of the country, and be impoverished or imprisoned without fault, or first cause, and the whole power of the government can be directed against him to crush him for maintaining to resist the wrong by demonstrating it or by appeal to the courts of justice; or when the courts hold laws valid the repeal the shameless audacity the solemn promises, pledges and contracts of the State, made to and with those under its protection and guardianship; or when those charged with offenses are tried by unconstitutional tribunals, were deprived of liberty without the

---

195 Quarles, *Enchiridion* (1641) 2.61
196 Quarles, *Enchiridion* (1641) 3.12–13
197 Quarles, *Enchiridion* (1641) 3.15
198 Diogenes Laërtius, *Solon*, 10, in Longe, trans., *Lives and Opinions* (1853), 28

process of law, and other expedients of tyranny, which is been familiar in all the ages are resorted to, to oppress and punish the citizen; and the souls of the people do not flame out with a just and fiery indignation at these wrongs, they become accomplices and justifiers of the tyranny and outrage, the public conscience is stupefied and lethargic in the soul of the state is stricken with paralysis.

Take heed rather what thou receivest, than what thou givest. What thou givest leaves thee, what thou takest sticks by thee: He that presents a gift, buys the receiver; he that takes a gift, sells his liberty.[199]

If thou hast providence to foresee a danger, let thy prudence rather prevent it than fear it. The fear of future evils brings oftentimes a present mischief: whilst thou seekest to prevent it, practice to bear it: he is a wise man that can avoid an evil, he is a patient man that can dure it, but he is a valiant man that can conquer it.[200]

Seest thou good days, prepare for evil times: no summer but hath its winter : he never reaped comfort in adversity, that sowed it not in prosperity.[201]

If thou desire to be wiser yet, think not thyself yet wise enough: and if thou desire to improve knowledge in thyself, despise not the instructions of another: he that instructs him that thinks himself wise enough, hath a fool to his scholar: he that thinks himself wise enough to instruct himself, hath a fool to his master.[202]

Censure no man, detract from no man: praise no man before his face; traduce no man behind his back. Boast not thyself abroad, nor flatter thyself at home: if anything cross thee, accuse thyself; if any one extol thee, humble thyself; honour those that instruct thee, and be thankful to those that reprehend thee. Let all thy desires be

---

[199] Quarles, *Enchiridion* (1641) 3.61
[200] Quarles, *Enchiridion* (1641) 3.64
[201] Quarles, *Enchiridion* (1641) 3.97
[202] Quarles, *Enchiridion* (1641) 3.100

subjected to reason, and let thy reason be corrected by religion. Weigh thyself by thy own balances, and trust not the voice of wild opinion: observe thyself as thy greatest enemy, so shalt thou become thy greatest friend.[203]

If thou desire the love of God and man, be humble; for the proud heart, as it loves none but itself, so it is beloved of none but by itself: the voice of humility is God's music, and the silence of humility is God's rhetoric. Humility enforces, where neither virtue nor strength can prevail, nor reason.[204]

Science by much is short of wisdom…. Knowledge is the treasurer of the mind; but discretion is the key, without which it lies dead, in the dullness of a fruitless rest…. The practical part of wisdom is the best. A native genius is beyond industrious study. Wisdom is no inheritance….[205]

Regard not in thy pilgrimage how difficult the passage is, but whether it tends; nor how delicate the journey is, but where it ends; if it be easy, suspect it; if hard, endure it; he that cannot excuse a bad way, accuseth his own sloth; and he that sticks in a bad passage, can never attain a good journey's end.[206]

A good resolution is the most fortifying armour that a discreet man can wear. That can defend him against all the unwelcome shuffles that the poor rude world puts on him. Without this, like hot iron, he hisses at every drop that finds him. With this, he can be a servant as well as a lord; and have the same inward pleasantness in the quakes and shakes of fortune, that he carries in her softest smiles…. That which puts the loose woven mind into a whirling tempest is by the resolute seen, slighted, laughed at; with as much honour, more quiet, more

---

[203] Quarles, *Enchiridion* (1641) 4.72
[204] Quarles, *Enchiridion* (1641) 4.54
[205] Felltham, *Resolves, Divine, Moral, and Political* (1677 ed.), 1.44
[206] Quarles, *Enchiridion* (1641) 3.30

safety. The world has nothing in it worthy a man's serious anger. The best way to perish discontentments, is either not to see them, or convert them to a dimpling mirth. How endless will be the quarrels of a choleric man; and the contentments of him that is resolved to turn indignities into things to make sport withal!

...In high and mountained fortunes resolution is necessary to ensafe us from the thefts and wiles of prosperity; which steal us away, not only from ourselves but virtue: and for the most part, like a long peace, softly delivers us into impoverishing war. In the wane of fortune resolution is likewise necessary, to guard us from the discontents that usually assail the poor dejected man. For all the world will beat the man whom Fortune buffets. And unless by this he can turn off the blows, he shall be sure to feel the greatest burthen in his own sad mind. A wise man makes a trouble less by fortitude; but to a fool, it is heavier by his stooping to it.... Honesty is a warrant of far more safety than fame: I will never be ashamed of that which bears her seal.... As for the crackers of the brain, and tongue-squibs, they will die alone, if I shall not revive them. The best way to have them forgotten by others is first to forget them myself.[207]

---

[207] Felltham, *Resolves, Divine, Moral, and Political* (1677 ed.), 1.2

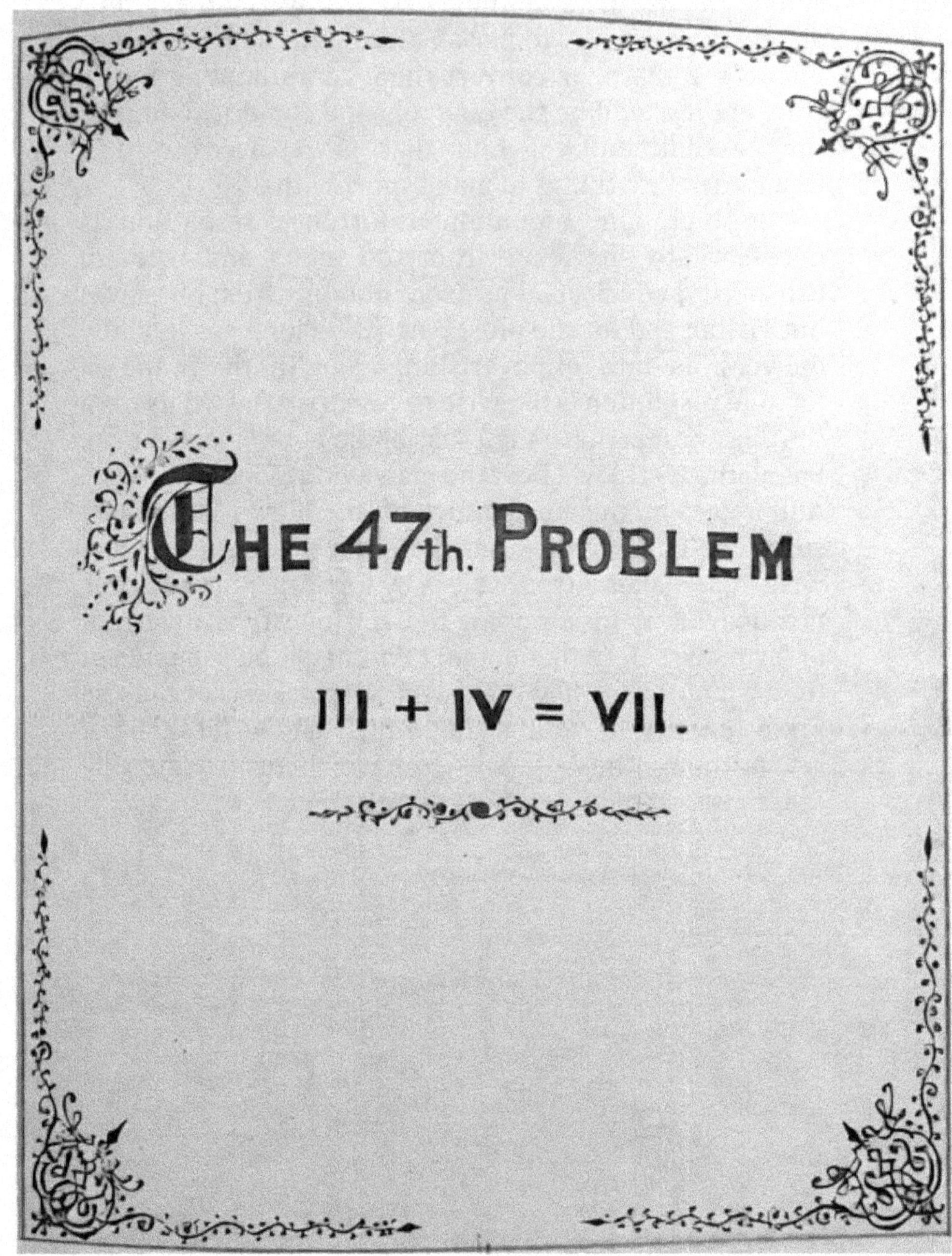
The 47th. Problem
III + IV = VII.

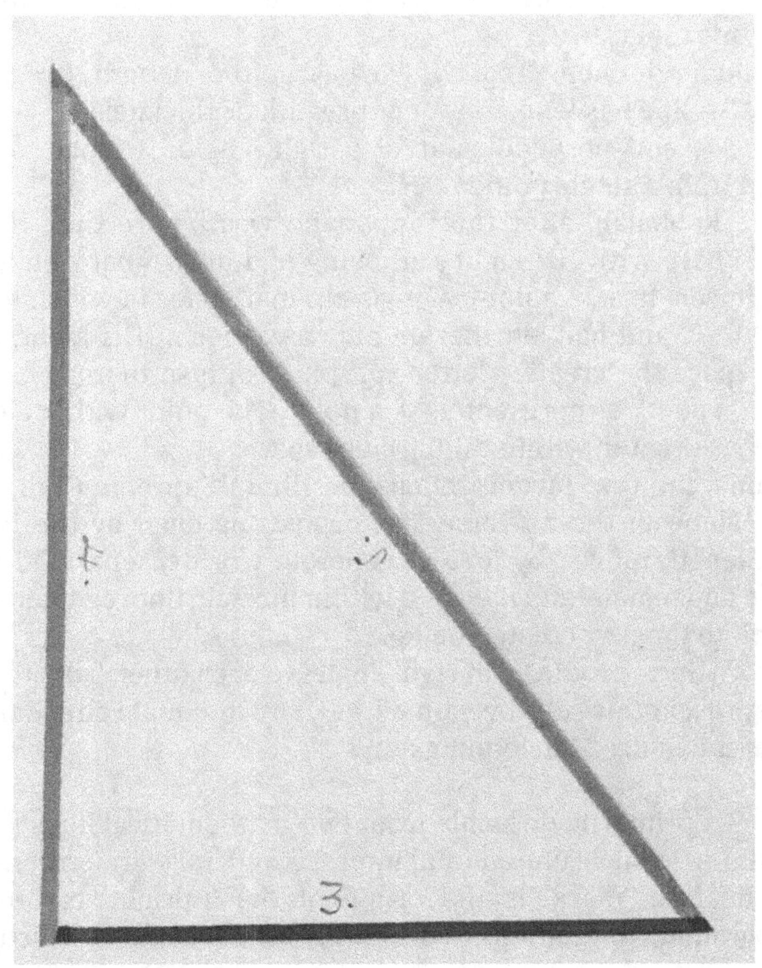
4
5
3.

THE 47TH PROBLEM

The 47th Problem of Euclid is, that the sum of the squares of the base and perpendicular of every right angled triangle is equal to the square of the hypotenuse.

The base representing *three* and the perpendicular *four*, the hypotenuse will represent five equal parts.

This figure appears on the tracing board of every Mason's lodge; and it is very seldom the case that any attempt is made to explain its symbolic meaning.

A point is defined, "that which has neither length, breadth nor thickness." A line has length, but not breadth or thickness.

The base and perpendicular of a right-angled triangle are lines projected from a single point.

In the Kabbalah, after the Deity, who was before then filled the whole of space with His Light and being had drawn back on all sides within himself, from a point leaving a circular space in which to create the worlds,[208] and had left therein only a vestige of His Light, he sent into the space the creative letter *yud* |י|, to diffuse there the creative Light; and *yud* |י| is represented as a point. The point within a circle is the Deity as Creator, within this circular space.

Brahma, the One Incomprehensible Hindu Supreme God, without sex, and alone in the universe, not cognizable even by the intellect, when at length moved by love to generate worlds, separated himself into male and female, and *maya*,[209] within himself, impregnated by him, gave birth to the first created being.

The two lines, produced at right angles to each other, from the single point, represent this self-division of the deity into male and female.

"All architecture," Mr. Jennings says,

> is primarily dirivable from two mathematical lines (|
> and —) which, united (and intersecting), form the 'cross.'
> The first 'mark' is the origin of the 'upright' tower,
> pyramid, or imitation ascending 'flame of fire,' which

---

[208] For Pike's overview of Lurianic Kabbalah's theory of cosmogony see Arturo de Hoyos, *Albert Pike's Morals and Dogma: Annotated Edition* (Washington, DC: Supreme Council, 33°, 2011, 2013), 28:702–81

[209] *Maya* (Sanskrit: माया), which literally means "magic" or "illusion," is the narrow mental and physical "reality" which we experience daily as living humans. What our consciousness perceives as "real" is rather an illusory construct in which we are entangled for the sake of sense-experience.

aspires against the force of gravity; also of the steeple, or phallus, all over the world. The second, or horizontal, 'mark' is the symbol of the tabernacle, chest, or ark, or fluent or base-line, which is the expression of all Egyptian, Grecian, and Jewish Templar architecture.[210]

Plato, in the Timæus, held that whatever is generated must proceed from some cause, namely God, who formed the sensible universe according to an eternal pattern existing in the divine mind. With him, matter is the receptacle, and, as it were, the nurse of production:—it is described as one and the same with space, which furnishes a place for all generated things. "This principle of nature, therefore, is without form,—without an *idea*; and it is only in the productions of the Creative Energy and the all-susceptible Nature— that is, in the Son of the Father and Mother, that there is form and determinate idea."[211]

"From the elements, four in number," he says,

> the universe was confessedly generated by a certain proportion ... the composition of the world receiving the entirety of each."[212] And, "From one essence indivisible, and always the same, and from another again that is divisible and corporeal, he composed by admixture from both a third form of *essence* intermediate between the two; and again, between what is indivisible and divisible as respects bodies, he placed the nature of *same* and *variable*, and taking these three, he mingled them all into one idea....[213]

As Plato thought that "Ideas" existent in the Divine Intellect were the cause of things being what they are, Pythagoras found these causes

---

[210] Hargrave Jennings, *The Rosicrucians, Their Rites and Mysteries; with Chapters on the Ancient Fire and Serpent-Worshippers, and Explanations of the Mystic Symbols Represented in the Monuments and Talismans of the Primeval Philosophers* (London: John Camden Hotten, 1870), 161

[211] August Heinrich Ritter, *Geschichte* der *Philosophie Alter Zeit* (1830) as translated and cited in Davis, *The Works of Plato.* [...] *vol. II.* (1849), 315

[212] Davis, *The Works of Plato* (1849) 2:336. Davis translates this "the composition of the world received one *whole* of each," but notes "Gr. ἓν ὅλον ἑκάστον,—one whole, without deficiency or superfluity, the τὸ τέλειον, alluded to by Aristotle, Metaph. iv. § 16." Note that Paul, 1 Corinthians 13:10, similarly uses the phrase τὸ τέλειον, "the perfect," to signify *complete*. This conveys a similar meaning to the Hebrew word *shelemut* (שלמות), "whole, complete, entire, perfect."

[213] Davis, *The Works of Plato* (1849) 2:339

in numbers; which, like necessity or fate, seemed to him to govern even the gods. For Pythagoreans invested particular numbers with extraordinary attributes, and applied them by very strange and forced analogies: and Mr. Thirlwall thinks that "the place which Pythagoras described to his numbers, is intelligible only by supposing that he confounded, first, a numerical unit with a geometrical point, and then this with a material atom."[214]

Every number had, with the Pythagoreans, meaning and among them "seven was a sacred number, as it had been considered from the earliest times. They called it a number of perfection, because composed of three and four, the triangle and the square, by which they said all things are capable of being measured; to them, therefore, it was the number of fitness, quantity, diversity, and perfection. It was also the number of life, because, according to their philosophy, it contained body and soul-body being of four elements and soul of three powers,"[215] rational, irascible, and concupiscible.

This number was sacred among the Hebrews and Egyptians. We do not find it so in the Vedas, but we do find there the seven stars of Ursa Major deified, and these being divisible into four and three. In the adoration of this group of stars we find the origin of the peculiar virtues ascribed to the number seven, among the Aryan races everywhere.

"Seven is what is called by arithmeticians a *prime* number, that is, it cannot be produced by the multiplication of the numbers. In the language of the Neo-Platonists, the number seven is said to be a virgin, and without a mother, and it is therefore sacred to Minerva."[216] Plato characterized "the particles of fire as pyramids, because they were sharp and tend upwards; and there of earth's cubes, because they are stable, and fill space."[217]

Plato, in *Timæus*, speaking of the two harmonic scales, as arranged by the Deity, says, "after dividing into six parts, and forming therefrom seven unequal circles, divided by double and triple intervals, three of each, he bade these circles travel in contrary directions to each other,—three of the seven to revolve at equal velocities, the remaining four with

---

214 William Whewell, *History of the Inductive Sciences from the Earliest to the Present Times.* 3d ed., 3 vols. (London: John W. Parker and Son, 1857), 1:47, quoting Dionysius Lardner, ed., *Cabinet Cyclopedia.* 133 vols., vol. II: *A History of Greece by the Rev. Connop Thirlwall* (Longman, Rees, Orme, Green & Longman, Paternoster-Row and John Taylor, 1836), 142

215 William Sidney Gibson, *Lectures and Essays on Various Subjects, Historical, Topographical, and Artistic* (London: Longmans and Co., 1858), 186

216 Whewell, *History of the Inductive Sciences* 3d ed. (1857), 1:223

217 Whewell, *History of the Inductive Sciences* 3d ed. (1857), 1:223

a velocity unequal as respects either of the former three, yet in a certain proportion as to their respective periods."[218]

The Semitic nations also attached mystical ideas to the numbers three, five and seven. The seven Cabiri of the Phoenicians were probably, at the beginning, the seven stars of Ursa Major. And these numbers curiously appear in the Semitic home of great antiquity, which giving an account of the trials of Ayūb, and recording the imaginary conversations of himself, his friends and the Deity himself, we call "The book of Job."

He had *seven* sons and *three* daughters; *seven* thousand sheep, and *three* hundred camels; *five* hundred yoke of oxen, and *five* hundred she-asses; and after his trials, he had *thrice* the number of animals of each kind, and, again, *seven* sons and *three* daughters. And these numbers, and 12 play an important part in the arrangements of the book.

In fact, the numbers 3, 4, 7, 10 and 12 were regarded by the Israelites as having a kind of sacred and important meaning, and after determine, in their writings, besides the groups of verses, the position of the names of God.[219] The Decalogue has its form determined by regard to number. "Genesis consists of 10 groups or books of narratives. David paid regard to the principle of numbers, even in his public arrangements. He divided the singers (1 Chron. 25), into 24 classes, each of 12 members, and the 24 was divided by 10 and 14. [...] In the first chapter of Isaiah, the representation made of the sinful revolt of the people is completed in the number 7, divided into 3 and 4,—4 designations for the idea of sinfulness, and 3 for that of revolt. So also do the designations applied in verse 6 to the miserable condition of the people, which their apostasy entailed upon them, make up the number 7, and the 7 is here again divided into 3 and 4."[220] Hengstenberg, |*Commentary on the Psalms,*| gives other examples of similar groupings.

---

[218] Davis, *The Works of Plato* (1849) 2:339

[219] "We shall now speak of the two Psalms in which there is found a mere approach to the alphabetical arrangement, Ps. ix., I. Notwithstanding the greatness of their deviations, the opinion has also been propounded in regard to them, that the alphabetical arrangement was there also originally preserved with exactness, and was only disturbed afterwards by negligence and caprice. But besides that this view proceeds upon an entirely false opinion of the state of the Heb. text generally, and, in particular, of that of the Psalms, the integrity of which is established by indisputable facts, such as the preservation of the names of God in their original position, and the arrangement according to the significant numbers...." —Rev. John Thomson and Rev. Patrick Fairbairn, trans., Ernst Wilhelm Hengstenberg, *Commentary on the Psalms* 2d ed. (Edinburgh: T. & T. Clark, 1860), vol. 3, append., 36

[220] Hengstenberg, *Commentary* (1860), vol. 3, append., 33

All important numbers are found in Psalms 9 and 10. In the two the name Jehovah occurs 14 times, Elohim 3 times; in Psalm 9 there are ten names of God, in Psalm 10, seven. All the significant numbers, too, are found in the two Psalms. The second part of Psalm 10 is completed in the number 7, manifestly on purpose. And "the interchange of the name Jehovah and Elohim was obviously managed so as to bring out for the whole the numbers 17 and 14, and for Psalm 10, the number 7."[221] Commonly, in the Psalms and Apocalypse, 7 is divided into 3 and 4. Hengstenberg gives instances of this from the Psalms.

In the Gospel according to John 21:2, is found,

> There were together Simon Peter, and Thomas called Didymus, and Nathaniel of Cana of Galilee, and the sons of Zebedee, and two others of his disciples." Here the number 7 is divided by the three and the four, as often is the case in the Apocalypse. At the head of the number 3, Peter; at the head of the number 4, the sons of Zebedee. It is only by grouping them thus, that we can explain the separation of the sons of Zebedee from Peter. The 7 are also divided by the 4,—Peter at the head, then three pairs. By the arrangement in pairs it is intimated that only the twos are rendered prominent, without any importance being attached to the separate names.[222]

In the 5 loaves and 2 fishes we find another division of 7. The Revelation or Apocalypse is addressed to the 7 Churches, from Christ, and the seven spirits before his throne. There were 7 golden candlesticks, and the Son of Man surrounded by them had in his right hand 7 stars. Round the throne (in chapter 4) were 25 Elders, and 7 lamps burning before it, which were the 7 spirits of God. The Book, in chapter 5, had 7 seals. The lamb that took it had seven horns and 7 eyes, the spirits of God, sent to all the earth. 144,000 were sealed, 12,000 from each tribe. 6 seals were opened in succession, and the 7th after an interval. 7 angels stood before God, having 7 trumpets. 7 thunders uttered their voices.

The Gentiles were to tread the city under foot 6 x 7 months, and the witnesses to prophecy 1260 (7 x 180) days. 7 thousand men were to be

---

[221] Hengstenberg, *Commentary* (1860), vol. 3, append., 37

[222] Rev. Patrick Fairbairn, trans., Ernst Wilhelm Hengstenberg, *The Revelation of St John: Expounded for Those who Search the Scriptures* 2 vols. (Edinburgh: T. & T. Clark, 1852), 2:450

slain by earthquake. The dragon has 7 heads and 10 horns and 7 crowns on his head; and the woman had on her head a crown of 5 + 7 stars. She was to be in the wilderness 1260 days, The beast that rose out of the sea had 7 heads and 10 horns and crowns, and continued 42 months. 7 angels had 7 plagues, and 7 golden vials of wrath. The beast on which the woman sat at 7 heads and 10 horns. There were 7 kings, 5 of whom had fallen. The wall of the city measured 144 cubits, and it had 12 gates, 3 on each side, it being square, and measuring 12,000 furlongs.

And Hengstenberg finds, in the addresses to the 7 churches many curious instances of the number 7, divided into 3 and 4.[223]

In the book Leviticus, the number 7 is often connected with the ceremonial. The Sabbath of rest was the 10th day of the 7th month: the oil of cleansing will sprinkle 7 times, and was the blood of the sacrificed bullock. 7 days was the period of uncleanliness, and lepers were secluded 7 days, and again 7 days. The number of lands to be offered for the whole people was, at almost every sacrifice, 7 or 14 (See Numbers 28 and 29).

It is entirely probable that, as I have already said, the peculiar significance of the number seven, is formed by three and four, at its origin in the worship of the seven stars of were so major which are naturally so divided. Afterward the reference was paid to the number itself, and mystical meanings were attached to it and its parts. Pythagoras may have formed his peculiar views in regard to numbers, upon what he learned in regard to them in Syria and Phoenicia, with the doctrines of whose priests he was familiar. His discovery of the necessary truth which is demonstrated in the 47th problem, gave him new views, and made the right angled triangle a symbol to him of what he regarded as the profound truths of philosophy.

He sacrificed a hecatomb, on discovering that truth; but Masonic writers should cease to say that he cried "Eureka." It was Archimedes who, "when he saw the water rising in the bath, as his body sank into it, rushed out crying 'I have found the way' [Εὕρηκα]. What he had found being the solution of the practical question of the quantity of silver mixed with the gold of Hiero's crown."[224]

Plutarch (*De Iside et Osiride*, 56) gives the following explanation of the symbolic meaning of the right angled triangle.

---

[223] Hengstenberg, *Revelation of St John* (1852) 1:151
[224] Whewell, *History of the Inductive Sciences* 3d ed. (1858) 2:243

Now *"universal nature,"* in its utmost and most perfect extent, may be considered as made up of these three things, of *Intelligence* [Νοντος, *nontos*], of *Matter* [Ὕλη, *húlē*], and of that which is the result of both these, in the Greek language, called *Kosmos* [Κοσμος], (a word which equally signifies either *beauty* and *order* or the *world* itself)— Νοντος |*Nontos*| be the same with what *Plato* is wont to call the *Idea*, the *Exemplar*, and *the Father*; to Ὕλη |*húlē*| he has given the name of the *Mother*, the *Nurse*, and the *Place* and *Receptacle of generation*; and to the *latter* of them, that of the *Off-spring*, and the *Production—so* again with regard to the Egyptians, there is good season to conclude, that they were wont to liken this *universal Nature* to, what they called, the most beautiful and perfect *Triangle*; the same, as does *Plato* himself in that *nuptial diagram*, as it is termed, which he has introduced into his *Republic*. Now in this *Triangle*, which is rectangular, the perpendicular side is imagined equal to three, the base to four, and the hypotenuse, which is equal to the other two containing sides, to five. In this scheme therefore we must suppose, that the Perpendicular is designed by them to represent the masculine nature, the Base the feminine, and that the Hypotenuse is to be looked upon as the off-spring of both: and accordingly, the *first* of them will aptly enough represent *Osiris* or the prime cause, the second, *Isis* of the receptive power, the last *Horus* or the common effect of the other two. For 3 is the first number which is composed of both even and odd; and *four* is a square whose fide is equal to the even number 2; but 5, being generated, as it were out of both the preceding numbers 2 and 3, may be laid to have an equal relation to both of them, as to its common parents. So again, the same word [Πάντα] which signifies the universe of beings, is of a similar found (in the Greek tongue) with this number [πεντε, five]; as *to count five,* in the same language, is sometimes made use of for *counting* in general [καὶ τὸ ἀριθμήσασθαι πεμπάσασθαι λέγουσιν]. But this number is still more regarded by the Egyptians, because, when multiplied into itself, it exactly equals the number of their letters, as well as makes up the summe of the years which the *Apis* lives. They are moreover wont to give *Horus* the name of *Kaimis,* by which word they mean *something which may be seen;* for this *World is* perceptible to the senses and visible. As to *Isis,* she is sometimes called by them *Muth,* sometimes *Athyri,* and at other times *Methuer.* Now the first of these names signifies *Mother,* the second, *Osiris's mundan habitation,* (or as *Plato* expresses it, the *place and receptacle of generation)* and the third is compounded of two other words, one of which imports *fullness,* and the other *goodness;* denoting hereby not only the fullness of the matter of which the world consists, but its intimate conjunction likewise with the good, the pure, and the well-ordered principle.[225]

The Pythagoreans, he informs us, appropriated the name "of *Apollo* to the *unit,* that of *Diana* to the *duad,* of *Minerva* to the *seven.*"[226]

"By *Osiris,*" he says, "therefore are we to understand those faculties of the universal *Soul,* such as intelligence and reason, which are, as it were, the supreme lords and directors of all that is good."[227]

Osiris, on the other hand, is designed by them under the hieroglyphic of *an eye and scepter;* the former denoting his providential wisdom, as the latter does upon does his power; wisdom and power being the two most distinguishing characteristics of the Deity.... Nor is it under mere symbols only that *Osiris* is represented to us; for we frequently meet with *statues* of him in the human shape, with his privy member erect; denoting hereby the mighty influence, which this God has in the production and support of all other beings."[228]

Isis therefore, according to our system, is the feminine part of nature, or that property of nature which renders her a fit

---

225 [Plutarch], *ΠΛΟΥΤΑΡΧΟΥ ΠΕΡΙ ΙΣΙΔΟΣ ΚΑΙ ΟΣΙΡΙΔΟΣ. Plutarchi De Iside et Osiride Liber: Graece et Anglice. Graeca Recensuit, Emendavit, Commentario Auxit Samuel Squire […] Accesserunt Xylandri, Baxteri, Marklandi, Conjecturae et Emendationes* (Cantabrigiae [Cambridge]: Typ. Academicis, 1744), 56 (pp. 78–79). Throughout his use of this text Pike makes occasional, minor, alterations/clarifications to the text, such as replacing "commonwealth" with "*Republic,*" and "vulgar" with "common."

226 Plutarch, *De Iside et Osiride,* 10, in Squire, *ΠΛΟΥΤΑΡΧΟΥ* (1744), 13

227 Plutarch, *De Iside et Osiride,* 49, in Squire, *ΠΛΟΥΤΑΡΧΟΥ* (1744), 68

228 Plutarch, *De Iside et Osiride,* 51, in Squire, *ΠΛΟΥΤΑΡΧΟΥ* (1744), 70–1

subject for the production of all other beings.... she is commonly called *Myriōnymus,* or the Goddess *with ten thousand Names*; denoting hereby that capability, with which she is endued, of receiving, and of being converted into all manner of forms and species, which it shall please the supreme Reason to impress upon her.[229]

Thus the perpendicular of the right-angled triangle represents the generated and creative power of the deity, of it would it was a symbol from its uprightness, precisely as the phallus, the stone column, the round tower in the obelisk were. It is the Divine Wisdom, by which he creates, and the Divine Potency of generation. Composed of three measures or equal parts, in one line, issuing and extended from the point, it is the Triune Deity: Creator, Preserver and Destroyer; and the base, composed of four like equal parts, is Isis or Nature, is Maya, created by Brahm within himself, by division of himself into male and female; is the productive, as the perpendicular is the generative. And these two are comprehended by their squares in the square of their issue and product, the universe of things and beings. To the Kabbalist, they are *hokmah,* the divine wisdom, or the intellectual potency to generate thought, and *daath,* the thinking or intellection, so generates and produced; and also the divine justice or severity |*gevurah*|, and benignity or mercy |*hesed*|, and the harmony or beauty |*tiferet*| that is the result of the two, in equilibrium.

The Fellow Craft is told that the seven liberal arts and sciences are grammar, rhetoric, logic, arithmetic, geometry, music and astronomy.

Of some of these, Plato discourses. By the sciences, he meant arithmetic, geometry, music in its theory, and astronomy; all of which were requisite for the study of true philosophy. In the sciences, every step is from beauty to beauty, for in every new theorem there is discovered something to attract by its intellectual charm, as the beauty of the body delights the eye; and thus each different science seems a different and a wider world of beauty.

We take the following extracts from *The Republic.*

> Number and unity "...lead and turn the soul to the contemplation of real being.... [A]ll computation and arithmetic concern numbers ... [and the philosopher]

---

[229] Plutarch, *De Iside et Osiride,* 53, in Squire, ΠΛΟΥΤΑΡΧΟΥ (1744), 74

must necessarily learn them ... with a view of understanding real being, after having emerged of the unstable condition of becoming or else he can never become an apt reasoner."[230] Those about to engage in the most important matters of ought matters to apply themselves to computation, and study it, not in the common vulgar fashion, but with the view of arriving at the contemplation of the nature of numbers by the intellect itself ... and that the soul may acquire a facility of turning itself from what is in course of generation to truth and real being."[231] [i.e., From the things that come into being and succeed each other, the transitory, the becoming, the phenomena, to the essence, substance and reality, that which IS, in the eternal laws of number and proportion that rule in every department of the universe, in the suns and worlds, the rainbow, the leaves, the vertebrae of animals, the crystals, the shields of the minute infusoria,[232] and the notes of the musical scale].

How refined is that branch of science "and in many ways useful to us as respects our wishes, if we will apply thereto for the sake of getting knowledge.... [I]t powerfully leads the soul upwards, and compels it to reason on abstract numbers[233] [αὐτοὶ ὁι ἀριθμοὶ, the very selves of numbers, which alone are the subject. One, the *monad*, is the idea of unity, abstract, invisible (αὐτο το ἔν, the one's very self), the *duad*, two, are divided into two, of abstract duality, &c.] without in any way allowing a person in his reasoning to advance numbers which are visible and tangible bodies [the concrete numbers (ἀριθμοὶ σώματα ἔχοντες, the numbers having bodies, or embodied), are the subjects only of everyday practical enumeration and computation. One *thing*, whatever that

---

[230] Plato, *The Republic*, 7.8, in Davis, *The Works of Plato* (1849) 2:214. Plato reads ἢ μηδέποτε λογιστικῷ γενέσθαι, which Paul Shorey, *Plato in Twelve Volumes* (1969) translates "or he can never become a true reckoner," which suggests more mathematical skill than philosophical insight.

[231] Plato, *The Republic*, 7.8, in Davis, *The Works of Plato* (1849) 2:214

[232] *Infusoria* are microscopic aquatic organisms, such as the ciliates, euglenoids, protozoa, unicellular algae, and small invertebrates in freshwater ponds.

[233] Plato reads αὐτῶν τῶν ἀριθμῶν, which Shorey, *Plato in Twelve Volumes* (1969), translates as "numbers (in) themselves," i.e., pure numbers.

may be, may be conceived of as divisible into parts, and therefore is being multiplied parts, which are things, forming an aggregate which is another thing; but abstract unity is not divisible into parts, having none in itself].[234]

These abstract numbers "can be comprehended by the intellect alone, and in no other way," Plato continues, "and our real need of this branch of science is probably because it seems to compel the soul to use pure intelligence in the search after pure truth."[235]

Of geometry, Plato says:

> [A]s for any considerable amount [of geometry and arithmetic,] and great progress in [the former], we must inquire how far they tend to ... make us apprehend more easily the idea of The Good ... to which all things contribute ... which compel the soul to turn itself to that region in which is the happiest portion of true being, which it must by all means perceive.... This science has an entirely opposite nature to the words employed in it by those who practice it.... [A]ll the terms they use seem to be with a view to operation and practice, such as squaring, producing, adding, and [the] like ... whereas ... the whole science should be studied [with a view to gain] ... real knowledge ... the knowledge of eternal being, and not of that which is subject to generation and destruction.... [I]t is the business of geometry to concern itself with eternal being. It would ... [tend] to draw the soul to truth, and to cause a philosophic intelligence to direct upwards the thoughts which we now improperly cast downwards.[236]

Of astronomy, he says:

> [B]y these branches of study, some organ of the soul in each individual, is purified and rekindled like fire, after having been destroyed and blinded by other kinds of

---

[234] Pike's two bracketed remarks borrow from a footnote by Davis, *The Works of Plato* (1849) 2:214–15

[235] Plato, *The Republic*, 7.8, in Davis, *The Works of Plato* (1849) 2:215

[236] Plato, *The Republic*, 7.9, in Davis, *Works of Plato* (1849) 2:216

study,—an organ, indeed, better with preserving than ten thousand eyes, since by it alone truth can be seen.... [It is astronomy] which compels us all to look upwards, and from what is here leads to there.... [But no] branch of science can make the soul look upward, except that which has to do with real being and the invisible ... and with that no one would will become acquainted by merely gazing upward, endeavoring to become familiar with any perceptible object.... He would never become acquainted with it, because the soul has no scientific knowledge of such things, nor would his soul look upward, but only downward, [however much he looked upward with his eyes].[237]

[T]hese various bright bodies in the heavens ... so variously placed in visible space, ought to be deemed very beautiful and most perfect in their kind, though much inferior to the true magnificence of movement, with which real velocity and real retardation mutually bear along those bodies with all that belongs to them, in their true number and in all their true forms, which things ... can be apprehended only by reason and intelligence, not by sight ... [We must] use the various heavenly phenomena, as an exhibition for the purpose of instructing us in [those realities as we should paintings of the same by a skillful artist].... [O]ne skilled in geometry, on seeing such drawings [might] think them to be exceedingly well [executed], and nevertheless deem it absurd to give them a serious consideration, as if he were thence to get his conception of truth about equals, or doubles, or any other proportion....[238]

So, Plato thinks, the true astronomer will regard to the stars, their orbits, as the work of the Divine Architect, without imagining that the proportions of time, is connected with the heavenly bodies, of night with day, and both these two a month, and of the month to a year, and of other stars to both of these portions of time, have always existed without change, solely because of, and by, the existence of the heavenly

---

237 Plato, *The Republic*, 7.10, in Davis, *Works of Plato* (1849) 2:217–19
238 Plato, *The Republic*, 7.11, in Davis, *Works of Plato* (1849) 2:219

bodies. Wherefore, he says, let us make use of problems in astronomy, as in geometry, and dismiss the heavenly bodies, if we intend really to get acquainted with astronomy, and render useful instead of useless that portion of the soul which is naturally intelligent.[239]

Of music, he says that there are two kinds of motion, one the counterpart of the other, one of the heavenly bodies, and the other of the harmony of these. He says, "As the eyes seem formed for studying astronomy, so do the ears seem formed for harmonious motions; and these seem to be twins sciences to one another, as also the Pythagoreans say."[240] "The true musicians ... do here just what the others did in astronomy; for they search for numbers, and the symphonies which they hear, but also they inquire what numbers are symphonies, and which are not, and the reason why they are either one or the other."[241]

If this plan of inquiry into all the matters spoken of, Plato says, "touches on their mutual communion and alliance, their correlation, and proves how they are usually related, it will contribute something to what is required, and our labor will not be fruitless...."[242] But all this is the in introduction only, to the strain itself, or dialectic science, by which, without the aid of the perceptive faculties, the endeavors by means of reason to obtain to a knowledge of individual and real being, of the self-existent, apprehending by intelligence what The Good itself is, and so arriving at the end of the intelligible.[243]

"No other method," he continues,

> can attempt to ascertain through a regular process the nature of each particular being; for all other arts respect either the opinions and desires of men, or generations and compositions, or are employed wholly in the study of what is generated and compounded: but as for those others, which we alleged to have some relation to being, as geometry, and its dependent sciences, we behold them, as if dreaming indeed about real existence, it being impossible to have a true vision, so long as they employ hypotheses and keep them immovable, without the power of accounting for their existence; for where the

---

239 Plato, *The Republic*, 7.11, in Davis, *Works of Plato* (1849) 2:220
240 Plato, *The Republic*, 7.12, in Davis, *Works of Plato* (1849) 2:220
241 Plato, *The Republic*, 7.12, in Davis, *Works of Plato* (1849) 2:221
242 Plato, *The Republic*, 7.13, in Davis, *Works of Plato* (1849) 2:23
243 Plato, *The Republic*, 7.12, in Davis, *Works of Plato* (1849) 2:22

starting-point is the unknown, and the conclusion and intermediate steps are connected with that unknown principle, how can any such kind of assent ever possibly become science?[244]

There are, he says, science and reflection, these being intelligence; and faith and conjecture, which are opinion. "Opinion is employed about generation, a phenomena, the succession of things that *become*; and intelligence about true being; true being bearing to generation (the self-existent to that which becomes) the same relation as intelligence to opinion, science to faith, and reflection to conjecture."[245] He is skilled in dialectics, who apprehends the reasons of the essence of each particular, and science attain to the knowledge of the Good.[246]

"The world is the measure of the invisible. What is above equals what is below," says the Tablet of Emerald of Hermes.[247] Plato will not concede the name of science to geometry and astronomy and music, or to any extent of knowledge of the visible phenomena of nature. Science is to know the cause, and the reason of being of the whole universe, to ascend from nature to God, The True God, one real Being. The magnitudes and movements of bodies are nothing, if we do not look beyond these. There is nothing wonderful or admirable in a machine, *as* a machine, unconnected with the universe. It is his intellect, and the plan formed in it, and revealed by machine, that are wonderful and admirable. The plan existed in his mind, before it was embodied and revealed in wood and iron.

---

[244] Plato, *The Republic*, 7.13, in Davis, *Works of Plato* (1849) 2:223

[245] Plato, *The Republic*, 7.14, in Davis, *Works of Plato* (1849) 2:224

[246] Plato, *The Republic*, 7.14, in Davis, *Works of Plato* (1849) 2:224

[247] "Tis true without lying, certain & most true. / That which is below is like that which is above & that which is above is like that which is below to do the miracle of one only thing / And as all things have been & arose from one by the mediation of one: so all things have their birth from this one thing by adaptation. / The Sun is its father, the moon its mother, the wind hath carried it in its belly, the earth is its course. The father of all perfection in the whole world is here. Its force or power is entire if it be converted into earth. / Separate thou the earth from the fire, the subtile from the gross sweetly with great indoustry. It ascends from the earth to the heaven & again it descends to the earth & receives the force of things superior & inferior. / By this means you shall have the glory of the whole world and thereby all obscurity shall fly from you. / Its force is above all force, for it vanquishes every subtile thing & penetrates every solid thing. / So was the world created. / From this are & do come admirable adaptations where of the means (or process) is here in this. / Hence I am called Hermes Trismegist, having the three parts of the philosophy of the whole world / That which I have said of the operation of the Sun is accomplished & ended." —Issac Newton's translation, *Keynes MS. 28*, King's College Library, Cambridge

The Deity is the true object of science. All His visible works are but infinitesimal effects of an infinite power.[248] The infusoria and the stars are like atoms of infinite littleness, compared with that. But the universe of things generated and which become, appear and vanish in the immense infinite of eternity and unlimited space, express invisible symbols like spoken or written words, the Divine thought and idea.

Plato refers all, even the harmonies in terms of music, to numbers and numerical proportion. These numbers, and all numerical proportions and ratios, of bodies, movement in time, are not inseparable from the bodies and phenomena, existing only with them and because of them: but existed before them, and the divine mind, and were the rule and law by which he made all that is. They are necessarily the expression of intelligence, and prove there is an intelligent author of all things.[249]

The seven colors of the rainbow, divided by three and four, the three primary and the four secondary, and the seven intervals of the musical octave, divided into tones and semi-tones, are of no more interest, by themselves, nor with seven stars divided in the same way, if any more, than seven leaves similarly arranged. The knowledge of phenomena, or familiarity with physics, makes us neither wiser nor better if we do not go beyond these, and by them attain the larger knowledge of the creation. Nearly to know the classification and names of flowers and

---

[248] "Science, wandering in error, struggles to remove God's Providence to a distance from us and the material Universe, and to substitute for its supervision and care and constant overseeing, what it calls Forces—Forces of Nature—Forces of Matter. It will not see that the Forces of Nature are the varied actions of God." —Arturo de Hoyos, *Albert Pike's Morals and Dogma: Annotated Edition* (Washington, DC: Supreme Council 33°, SJ, 2011), 29:28

[249] "Today there is a wide measure of agreement, which on the physical side of science approaches almost to unanimity, that the stream of knowledge is heading towards a non-mechanical reality; the universe begins to look more like a great thought than like a great machine. Mind no longer appears as an accidental intruder into realm of matter; we are beginning to suspect that we ought rather to hail it as the creator and governor of the realm of matter—not of course our individual minds, but the mind in which the atoms out of which our individual minds have grown exist as thoughts. The new knowledge compels us to revise our hasty first impressions that we had stumbled into a universe which either did not concern itself with life or was actively hostile to life. The old dualism of mind and matter, which was mainly responsible for the supposed hostility, seems likely to disappear, not through matter becoming in any way more shadowy or insubstantial than heretofore, or through mind becoming resolved into a function of the working of matter, but through substantial matter resolving itself into a creation and manifestation of mind. We discover that the universe shews evidence of a designing or controlling power that has something in common with our own individual minds—not, so far as we have discovered, emotion, morality, or aesthetic appreciation, but the tendency to think in the way which, for want of a better word, we describe as mathematical." —Sir James Hopwood Jeans, *The Mysterious Universe* (Cambridge University Press, 1931), 137–38

plants and of crystals, is not true science, any more than it is science to know and distinguish and be familiar with the names of all the tiny creatures discovered by the microscope. The true science consists in knowledge of the Deity; as it is man himself, and not his words and works, that are the true objects of inquiry of the student of human nature.

"In all things," Plato says, in *The Timæus*, "we should inquire after the divine cause, with the view of obtaining a blessed life in the highest degree of which our nature admits; for the sake of which, also, we should investigate the necessary cause[250] as well,—convinced that, without these two classes of causes, which can neither understand nor apprehend, nor otherwise engage in the several objects of our anxious pursuit."[251]

"The grand doctrine of Theism," set forth in *The Timæus*, "is, whatever is generated must proceed from some cause, God, who formed the sensible universe, the most perfect of things generated, according to an eternal pattern existing in the Divine Mind. The whole being the work of the Creator's goodness,"[252] the very thought itself; and his notion, like that of Pythagoras, was, "that *numbers* and *music* are the principles of entire universe, and that the world is regulated by *numerical harmony*."[253] In the summary of this doctrine is, that "this world, which comprises and is filled with all kinds of living beings, both mortal and immortal, thus become visible animal, embracing visible natures,—an image of the great intelligence, a sensible God, the greatest and best, the fairest and most perfect, this, the one and only begotten universe."

He says, "that is which is *ever-existent,* [having] no generation ... is apprehended by reflection united with reason, always subsists [always the same]."[254] Its essence is to Be, and to be always one and the same. That, on the contrary, which is in a state of generation or becoming, never really *is*. Whatever is generated and exists, has a cause. "To discover then the *Creator* and *Father* of this [generated] universe, as well as his work, is ... difficult; and when discovered, it is impossible to

---

[250] Thomas Henri Martin, *Études sur le Timée de Platon* 2 vols. (Paris: Ladrange Libraire-Éditeur, 1841–42), 1:244 bis, as translated and quoted in Davis, "Introduction to *The Timæus*," in *The Works of Plato* (1849) 2:318

[251] Plato, *The Timæus*, 43, in Davis, *Works of Plato* (1849) 2:379

[252] Davis, "Introduction to *The Timæus*," in *Works of Plato* (1849) 2:314–15

[253] Davis, "Introduction to *The Timæus*," in *Works of Plato* (1849) 2:314

[254] Plato, *The Timæus*, 9, in Davis, *Works of Plato* (1849) 2:332

reveal him to mankind at large."[255] Generated by an eternal pattern, ever changeless, "it has been framed according to principles that can be comprehended by reason and reflection, and never abides in sameness of being…. [It] must necessarily be the resemblance of something…. The image must resemble its pattern and precisely as essence or true being is to generation, so is truth or faith (or conjecture)."[256]

We learn from Iamblichus, *Life of Pythagoras*, that Mnesarchus and Pythias, the parents of Pythagoras, resided in the city of Samos, upon the island of the same name, near the coast of the Aegean Sea, not far from Ephesus and Miletus.

A certain Samian poet says that Pythagoras was the son of Apollo. For thus he sings,

> *Pythias, fairest of the Samian tribe,*
> *Bore from the embraces of the God of day,*
> *Renowned Pythagoras, the friend of Jove.*

It is worth while, however, to relate how this report became so prevalent. The Pythian oracle [the oracle of Apollo Pythias] then had predicted to this Mnesarchus (who came to Delphi for the purposes of merchandize, with his wife not yet apparently pregnant, and who inquired of the God concerning the event of his voyage to Syria) that his voyage would be lucrative and most conformable to his wishes, but that his wife was now pregnant, and would bring forth a son surpassing in beauty and wisdom all that ever lived, and who would be of the greatest advantage to the human race in every thing pertaining to the life of man. But, when Mnesarchus considered with himself, that the God, without being interrogated concerning his son, had informed him by an oracle, that he would possess an illustrious prerogative, and a gift truly divine, he immediately named his wife Pythaïs, from her son and the Delphic prophet, instead of Parthenis, which was her former appellation; and he called the infant, who was soon after born at Sidon [Tsidūn] in Phoenicia, Pythagoras; signifying by this appellation, that such an offspring was predicted to him by the Pythian Apollo…. Indeed, no one can

---

255 Plato, *The Timæus*, 9, in Davis, *Works of Plato* (1849) 2:332
256 Plato, *The Timæus*, 9, in Davis, *Works of Plato* (1849) 2:333

doubt that the soul of Pythagoras was sent to mankind from the empire of Apollo, either being an attendant on the God, or co-arranged with him in some other more familiar way: for this may be inferred both from his birth, and the all-various wisdom of his soul.[257]

Iamblichus further informed us that Pythagoras was educated by Creophilus, by Pherecydes the Syrian, and others who presided over sacred concerns, at Samos, and came to be referenced and honored, even by elderly men, while yet a youth being "fortunately the most beautiful and godlike of all those that have been celebrated in the annals of history."[258] His great renown reached Thales at Miletus and Bias at Priēnē, men illustrious for their wisdom, and extended to the neighboring cities. He "was everywhere celebrated as the *long-haired Samian*, and was referenced by the multitude as one under the influence of divine inspiration."[259] "It was reasonably asserted by many that he was a son of God" and "he dwelt at Samos like some beneficent dæmon."[260]

At about the age of eighteen years he left Samos, and associated with Pherecydes, Anaximander and Thales at Miletus, "all [of whom] loved him, admired his natural endowments, and made him a partaker of their doctrines." Thales advised "him to sail into Egypt, and associate with the Memphian and Diospolitan Priests,"[261] and he, accepting this advice, sailed to Tsidūn, and there "conversed with the prophets who were the descendants of Mochus the physiologist, and with [other prophets] and ... with Phoenician Hierophants."[262] "He was likewise initiated in all the mysteries of Byblus and Tyre, and in the sacred operations which are performed in many parts of Syria."[263] Then he went by sea to Egypt, in an Egyptian vessel, which had come into port in Phoenicia, under Mount Caramel, in the temple where, he, separated for the most part, from all society, had been residing.

---

[257] Thomas Taylor, *Iamblichus' Life of Pythagoras, or Pythagoric Life. Accompanied by Fragments of the Ethical Writings of Certain Pythagoreans in the Doric Dialect; and a Collection of Pythagoric Sentences from Stobæus and Others, which are Omitted by Gale in his Opuscula Mythologica, and Have Not Been Noticed by any Editor. Translated from the Greek.* (London: A. J. Valpy, 1818), 3–6

[258] Taylor, *Iamblichus' Life of Pythagoras* (1818), 6

[259] Taylor, *Iamblichus' Life of Pythagoras* (1818), 7

[260] Taylor, *Iamblichus' Life of Pythagoras* (1818), 7

[261] Taylor, *Iamblichus' Life of Pythagoras* (1818), 8

[262] Taylor, *Iamblichus' Life of Pythagoras* (1818), 9

[263] Taylor, *Iamblichus' Life of Pythagoras* (1818), 9

Reaching Egypt, "he frequented all the Egyptian temples with the greatest diligence and with accurate investigation, [and] was both admired and loved by the priests and prophets with whom he associated.... [H]e went to all the priests, by whom he was furnished with the wisdom which each possessed. He spent therefore two and twenty years in Egypt, in the adyta of temples, astronomizing and geometrizing, and was initiated, not in a superficial or casual manner, in all the mysteries of the Gods, till at length being taken captive by the soldiers of Cambyses, he was brought to Babylon. Here he gladly associated with the Magi, was instructed by them in their venerable knowledge, and learnt from them the most perfect worship of the Gods. Through their assistance likewise, he arrived at the summit of arithmetic, music, and other disciplines; and after associating with them twelve years, he returned to Samos about the fifty-sixth year of his age."[264]

At Samos he endeavored, with little success to introduce the symbolical method of teaching, which he had learned in Egypt. Then he went to Delos, and worshiped there at the oracle of Apollo. He went to all the other oracles, and "dwelt for some time at Crete and Sparta ... becoming acquainted with their laws," and then returned to Samos, and established a school there, forming "a cavern out of the city, adopted to his philosophy, in which he spent the greater part, both of the day and the night."[265] "He was now admired by all Greece, and the best of those who philosophized came to Samos on his account, that they might participate of his erudition. The citizens likewise employed him in all their embassies, and compelled him to unite with them in the administration of public affairs."[266] However, finding these engagements incompatible with his philosophical pursuits, he went to Italy, and at Crotona had six hundred disciples, who not only devoted themselves to the study of philosophy, but amicably divided the goods of life in common; and thence acquired the appellation of *Cænobitæ*. Two thousand of his auditors, called *Acusmatici*, with their wives and children "founded a place which was universally called Magna Græcia. This great multitude of people likewise, receiving laws and mandates from Pythagoras as so many divine precepts, and without which they engaged in to occupation, dwelt together with the greatest general concord, celebrated and ranked by their neighbors among the number

---

264 Taylor, *Iamblichus' Life of Pythagoras* (1818), 12–13
265 Taylor, *Iamblichus' Life of Pythagoras* (1818), 16
266 Taylor, *Iamblichus' Life of Pythagoras* (1818), 17

of the blessed. At the same time, as we have already observed, they shared their possessions in common. Such also was their reverence for Pythagoras, that they numbered him with the Gods, as a certain beneficent and most philanthropic dæmon."[267]

He inspired the people of Italy and Sicily, and restored to independence and liberated many cities for which he established laws. He went to Italy in the 62d Olympiad (532–29 B.C.).

Diogenes Laërtius informs us that Heraclitus makes him the son of Mnesarchus, and a native of Samos, while Aristoxenus asserts that he was "a Tyrrhenian, and a native of one of the islands which the Athenians occupied, after they had driven out the Tyrrhenians."[268] Other writers say he was the son of Marmacus, descendant of an exilefrom Phlias, who settled in Samos, whence Pythagoras migrated to Lesbos, with letters to Pherecydes, whose pupil he became, and after his death returned to Samos, and became a pupil of Hermodamus.[269]

> And as he was a young man, and devoted to learning, he quitted his country, and got initiated into all the Grecian and barbarian sacred mysteries. Accordingly, he went to Egypt, on which occasion Polycrates gave him a letter of introduction to Amasis; and he learnt the Egyptian language, as Antipho tells us, in his treatise on those men who have been conspicuous for virtue, and he associated with the Chaldaeans and with the Magi.
>
> Afterwards he went to Crete, and in company with Epimenides, he descended into the En cave, (and in Egypt too, he entered into the holiest parts of their temples) and learned all the most secret mysteries that relate to their Gods.[270]

He claimed to have been, and to recollect to have been, in succession, Æthalides, accounted son of Mercury, Euphorbus, who was wounded by Menelaus, Hermotimus, Pyrrhus, a fisherman of Delos, and then to have become Pythagoras.[271]

---

267 Taylor, *Iamblichus' Life of Pythagoras* (1818), 17–18
268 Laërtius, *Life of Pythagoras*, 1, in Longe, *Lives and Opinions* (1853), 338
269 Laërtius, *Life of Pythagoras*, 4, in Longe, *Lives and Opinions* (1853), 340
270 Laërtius Laërtius, *Life of Pythagoras*, 3, in Longe, *Lives and Opinions* (1853), 338
271 Laërtius, *Life of Pythagoras*, 4, in Longe, *Lives and Opinions* (1853), 339–40

He wrote many books, three of which were extant in the time of Diogenes Laërtius, and many others, then extant, were falsely attributed to him.

"He [forbade] men to pray for anything in particular for themselves, because they could not know what is good for them."[272] "He asserted that the property of friends is common, and that friendship is equality."[273]

"He carried geometry to perfection, after Mœris had first found out the principles of the elements of that science,"[274] and the part of the science to which he applied himself above all others, was that of numbers. "And Apollodorus, the logician, records of him, that he sacrificed a hecatomb, when he had discovered that the square of the hypothenuse of a right-angled triangle is equal to the squares of the sides containing the right angle."[275]

"[I]f he ever heard that any one had a community of symbols with him, he at once made him a companion and friend."[276] "[W]hat he called his 'symbols,' were such as these: 'Do not stir the fire with the sword,' 'Do not bear the image of God on a ring,' 'Do not aid men is discarding a burden,' 'Do not offer your right hand lightly,' 'Do not cherish swallows under your roof.'"[277] He said that every man ought so to conduct himself, as to be worthy of belief without an oath.

He said "that the monad was the beginning of everything, from the monad proceeds an indefinite duad, which is subordinate to the monad as to its cause. That from the monad and the indefinite duad proceed numbers."[278] "The sun, moon and stars," he held, "were all Gods; for in them the warm principal predominated, which is the cause of life ... that there is a relationship between men and the Gods, because men partake

---

272 Laërtius, *Life of Pythagoras*, 6, in Longe, *Lives and Opinions* (1853), 341

273 Laërtius, *Life of Pythagoras*, 8, in Longe, *Lives and Opinions* (1853), 342

274 Laërtius, *Life of Pythagoras*, 11, in Longe, *Lives and Opinions* (1853), 342–3

275 Laërtius, *Life of Pythagoras*, 11, in Longe, *Lives and Opinions* (1853), 343

276 Laërtius, *Life of Pythagoras*, 16, in Longe, *Lives and Opinions* (1853), 345

277 Laërtius, *Life of Pythagoras*, 17, in Longe, *Lives and Opinions* (1853), 345–6. In *Esoterika* (2005), 175, Pike calls these "trite phrases with concealed meanings." Laërtius interprets several of these, writing, "Now the precept not to stir fire with a sword meant, not to provoke the anger or swelling pride of powerful men; not to violate the beam of the balance meant, not to transgress fairness and justice; not to sit on a bushel is to have an equal care for the present and for the future, for by the bushel is meant one's daily food. By not devouring one's heart, he intended to show that we ought not to waste away our souls with grief and sorrow. In the precept that a man when travelling abroad should not turn his eyes back, he recommended those who were departing from life not to be desirous to live, and not to be too much attracted by the pleasures here on earth. And the other symbols may be explained in a similar manner, that we may not be too prolix here."

278 Laërtius, *Life of Pythagoras*, 19, in Longe, *Lives and Opinions* (1853), 348

of the divine principle; on which account, also, God exercises his providence for our advantage.... And that the soul is different from life, [and] is immortal."[279]

He also says that the soul of man is divided into three parts: νοῦς [noûs], φρὴν [phrēn], and θυμὸς [thūmós], *intuition*, *reason* and *mind*, the first and third of which other animals had; that θυμὸς [thūmós], *reason*, had its seat in the heart, but the others resided in the brain.[280]

Nourrisson, *Progrès de la Pensée Humaine*, thus expounds the Pythagorean doctrine in regard to numbers:

> All objects can be numbered, and their relations in time and space, expressed by numbers. To this mathematical side of things, Pythagoras attached himself. Unity, or the monad, is for him the principal of all that is. Going forth from itself, the monitor engenders the duad, and returning upon itself, the triad. The number *four*, the tetractys or quaternary, or, again, the decad, because it is the sum of the four first numbers, is the sacred number, force of expansion and the source of life.
>
> Such as the basis on which rest the Pythagorean physics, the theodicy, and psychology.
>
> The monad is a point, which added to itself gives the line; a third point engenders surface, and a fourth, superposited on the three first, the pyramid or solid. The pyramid is the fire; the cube, the earth; the octahedron, the air; and the icosahedron, the water.... The unit *par excellance* is the Very God, "Who embraces all, provides for all and is the Only True One," the primitive element, which, longng for the void, divides itself into unities, at intervals determined by the three dimensions ... the Supreme Being, whence proceed all beings, demons, heroes and men.[281]

"What is the wisest thing? Number," was an audition of Pythagoras. And Iamblichus says "The mode ... of teaching through symbols, was considered by Pythagoras as most necessary. For this form of erudition was cultivated by nearly all the Greeks, as being most ancient. But it was

---

[279] Laërtius, *Life of Pythagoras*, 19, in Longe, *Lives and Opinions* (1853), 349

[280] Laërtius, *Life of Pythagoras*, 19, in Longe, *Lives and Opinions* (1853), 350

[281] [Jean-Félix] Nourrisson, *Tableau de Progrès de la Pensée Humaine depuis Thalès jusqu'a Leibniz* (Paris: Didier et Cie, 1858, 20–1

transcendently honored by the Egyptians, and adopted by them in the most diversified manner...."[282] All the disciples of Pythagoras, and, indeed, all of that age, he says "adopted this mode of teaching, in their discourses with each other, and in their commentaries and conversations. Their writings also, and all the books which they published, most of which have been preserved even to our time, were not composed by them in a popular and vulgar diction, and in a manner usual with all other writers, so as to be immediately understood, but in such a way as not to be easily apprehended by those that read them. For they adopted that taciturnity which was instituted by Pythagoras as a law, in concealing after an arcane mode, divine mysteries from the uninitiated, and obscuring their writings and conferences with each other. ... 'Sacrifice and adore unshod. Declining from the public ways, walk in unfrequented paths. Speak not about Pythagoric concerns without light,'"[283] are other of the symbolic sayings of these philosophers.

In the *Sacred Discourse* or *Treatise Concerning the Gods*, either written by Pythagoras himself, or by Telanges, being taken by him from commentaries left by Pythagoras to his daughter, the sister of Telanges, it is said, "that Pythagoras the son of Mnesarchus was instructed in what pertains to the Gods, when he celebrated orgies in the Thracian Libethra, being initiated in them by Aglaophemus; and that Orpheus the son of Calliope, having learnt wisdom from his mother in the mountain Pangaus, said, that the eternal essence of number is the most providential principle of the universe, of heaven and earth, and the intermediate nature ; and further still, that it is the root of the permanency of divine natures, of Gods and dæmons."[284]

"From these things," Iamblichus says, "therefore, it is evident that he learned from the Orphic writers that the essence of the Gods is defined by number. Through the same numbers also, he produced an admirable fore-knowledge and worship of the gods, both of which most allied to numbers." He furnished Abaris "with a consummate knowlo065cdge of all truth, as it is said, through the arithmetical science."[285]

Syrianus, *In Aristot[elis]. Metaphys[icorum]*., lib[er]. 13, says that "the Pythagoreans received from the theology of Orpheans, the principles of intelligible and intellectual numbers, assigned them an

---

282 Taylor, *Iamblichus' Life of Pythagoras* (1818), 75
283 Taylor, *Iamblichus' Life of Pythagoras* (1818), 76–7
284 Taylor, *Iamblichus' Life of Pythagoras* (1818), 105–6
285 Taylor, *Iamblichus' Life of Pythagoras* (1818), 107

abundant progression, and extended their dominion as far as to [things cognizable by the senses]. Hence that proverb was peculiar to the Pythagoreans, that 'all things are assimilated to number.' Pythagoras, therefore, in *The Sacred Discourse*, clearly says, that 'number is the ruler of forms and ideas, and is the cause of Gods and dæmons.' He also supposes, that 'to the most ancient and artificially ruling deity, number is the canon, the artificial reason, the intellect also, and the most undeviating balance of the composition and generation of all things."[286]

The "artificially ruling deity," as Taylor translates the phrase κρατιστευοντι τεχνίτη θεω [*kratistevonti techníti theo*], is the Deity as Artist or Artificer (the Grand Architect), establishing, and the "artificial reason," *logon technicon* [λογον τεχνικον] is the Divine Word or Reason or Artificer.

Syrianus adds, "But Philolaus declared that number is the governing and self-begotten concatenation [συοχήν, *syochín*] of eternal permanency of kosmic natures."[287]

And Hippasus, and all those who were destined to a five years' silence, called number the judiciary organ of the kosmingic God, and the primal exemplar of world-making.[288]

But how is it possible they could have spoken thus superlatively of number, unless they had considered it as possessing an essence independent of things cognizable by the senses, and in transcending at the same time fabricative and archetypal.[289]

An oath like the following is ascribed to the Pythagoreans, in which "him" was Pythagoras:

"I swear by him who the Tetractys found,
"Whence all our wisdom flows, and which contains
"Perennial Nature's fountain, cause and root."[290]

---

[286] Taylor, *Iamblichus' Life of Pythagoras* (1818), 106, reads, "as far as to sensibles themselves."

[287] The word συνοχή (synochí), which Taylor translates "bond," also means cohesion. Pike's use of concatenation, in mathematics, refers to the joining of numerals into a string, e.g., 1959 and 70 become 195970.

[288] Taylor translates this "And Hippasus, and all those who were destined to a quinquennial silence, called number the judicial instrument of the maker of the universe, and the first paradigm of mundane fabrication." —*Iamblichus' Life of Pythagoras* (1818), 106

[289] Taylor, *Iamblichus' Life of Pythagoras* (1818), 106–7

[290] Taylor, *Iamblichus' Life of Pythagoras* (1818), 109

"He ... ordained that men should make libations thrice and observed that Apollo delivered oracles on the tripod, because Triad is the first number."[291] "And he ordered that temples should be entered from places on the right hand, and that they should be departed out from the left hand. For he that asserted the right hand is the principle of what is called the odd number, and is divine; but that the left hand is as symbol of the even number, and that which is liable to dissolution."[292]

Two other of his symbolical sayings, quoted by Iamblichus, were "The beginning is the half of the whole," and "All things accord in number."[293]

The Pythagoreans, he says, "perpetually exhorted each other, not to [thrust out] the God [that was] within them. Hence all the endeavor of their friendship both in deeds and words, was directed to a certain divine mixture, to a union with Divinity, and to a communion with intellect and a divine soul."[294]

Proclus said, "The Monad is extended which generates Two." The Chinese say, "The Tao has produced One, One has produced Two, Two have produced Three, Three have produced all things." This is the Pythagorean Monad from the One, the Duad (Spirit and Matter), the Triad (their union in the kosmos)."[295]

"All things are established in the vision of this Triad."
"For in the whole world shines a Trial, over which a Monad rules."[296]

Plato said that the beginnings were God, and matter, and model (the soul of the world—the archetype).[297] Everything that is created, or becomes, is produced according to an Eternal pattern, the Ideal world,

---

291 Taylor, *Iamblichus' Life of Pythagoras* (1818), 111

292 Taylor, *Iamblichus' Life of Pythagoras* (1818), 113

293 Taylor, *Iamblichus' Life of Pythagoras* (1818), 118

294 Taylor, *Iamblichus' Life of Pythagoras* (1818), 170

295 S[amuel]. F[ales]. Dunlap, *Vestiges of the Spirit-history of Man* (New York: D. Appleton and Company, 1858), 150. The phrase "The Monad is extended which generates Two" is the twenty-sixth of the "Chaldæan Oracles of Zoroaster," in [James Russell Lowell], *The Phenix: A Collection of Old and Rare Fragments* [...] (New York: W. Gowan, 1835), 150. Proclus does not claim credit, but rather said, "For unity, according to the oracle, is extended and generates two...." See Thomas Taylor, *The Philosophical and Mathematical Commentaries of Proclus, on the First Book of Euclid's Elements. To which are Added, a History of the Restoration of Platonic Theology, by the Latter Platonists: and a Translation from the Greek of Proclus's Theological Elements* 2 vols. (London: Printed for the Author, 1792), 1:124

296 Chaldæan Oracles 31, 36, in Lowell, *The Phenix* (1835), 151

297 Lowell, *The Phenix* (1835), 184

the universe that is to exist,[298] perceived by and existing in the Divine Intellect. Before the material universe existed, there were God the Creator, idea, and matter. The universe is the utterance of the Divine Thought, the expression of the Divine idea. Here is the Zarathustrian Triad: Thought, Word, Deed.

According to Plato, the divine nature consists of three: — thought, the father; matter, the mother; Kosmos, the universe in the idea, the son. The reason of God is the where of this ideal or intelligible world.

"Everything generated," Proclus says, "requires matter and an efficient cause."[299]

Three is the symbol of and represents the deity as creator, the divine triad of father, mother, and "first begotten," the Monogenes, the Demiurge, the Word, Logos, or Wisdom. And four is the symbol of and represents matter; or the four elements, fire, air, earth, and water.

"The Divine Artist," Proclus says, "makes his proper matter, either giving subsistence to matter itself, or causing it to be adapted to his purpose.... Since, therefore, the artificer of the universe is also the artificer of matter, which is defined to be the receptacle and nurse of generation, he likewise made it to be the receptacle of generation."[300]

Heraclitus said, "strife is the father of things"; and "the one, setting itself at variance with itself, harmonizes with itself, like the harmony of the bow and the viol." "Unite," [he said], "the whole and the not-whole, the coalescing and the not-coalescing, the harmonious and the discordant, and thus we have the one becoming from the all, and the all from the one."[301]

According to Plato, there were "before the creation of the world, a Creator as a moving and a reflecting principle, with on the one side the ideal world existing immovable as the eternal archetype, and on the other side, a chaotic, formless, irregular, fluctuating mass, which holds in itself the germ of the material world, but has no determined character nor substance. With these two elements the Creator now blends the world-soul which he distributes according to the relation of numbers, and sets it in definite and harmonious motion."[302]

---

[298] Lowell, *The Phenix* (1835), 187

[299] Thomas Taylor, *The Fragments that Remain of the Last Writings of Proclus, Surnamed the Platonic Successor. Translated from the Greek.* (London: Printed for the Author, 1825), 58

[300] Taylor, *The Fragments that Remain of the Last Writings of Proclus* [...] (1825), 64–5

[301] Julius H. Seeyle, trans., Albert Schwegler, *A History Of Philosophy in Epitome* (New York and London: Appleton and Company, 1856), 33

[302] Schwegler, *A History Of Philosophy* (1856), 97

"That branch of science which concerns computation," Plato says, in *The Republic*, "powerfully leads the soul upwards, and compels it to reason on abstract numbers, without in any way allowing a cannot make it to be so that there can be right-angled triangles were sides will not be to each other in that proportion."

Pythagoras had thus found a striking confirmation of his theory as to numbers. And he found, not only that the relations are proportions of numbers, as applied to figures, were inflexible and unvarying, but that regard had been had to particular numbers, by the Creative Wisdom, in framing the universe. Modern science has discovered this creative regard for particular numbers, everywhere. There are seven rays, and colors manifested by them, in the white rays of the sun, when one of these passes through a prism, and of these seven, three are primary, and four secondary colors. There is a singular coincidence between these divisions of a ray of light, and the musical octave. The curious phenomena of crystallization are controlled by certain inflexible laws of number of proportion, that never vary in crystals of one and the same kind, though they are very different, as to those of different kinds. All the chemical compositions observed in the mineral kingdom follow the law deafened portions. Two substances may, indeedperson in his reasoning to advance numbers which are visible and tangible bodies.... [T]hey speak of such numbers only—as can be comprehended by the intellect alone...."[303]

> "There are three forms," he says, "from which all measures are composed, just as there are four primitive sounds, from which harmony is derived...."[304]

The great idea of Pythagoras was, the science of nature must clothe its conclusions in the language of mathematics. He believed, as Plato did, after him, there must be mathematical laws of nature; that it was the business of philosophy to discover those laws, and that though the will of the deity had created the universe in accordance with them, and made it to be governed by them, his will had not enacted those laws, and the proportions and relations of numbers; but the numbers themselves into these proportions and relations, were self-existent, and not even Omnipotence could annihilate them.

---

[303] Plato, *The Republic* 7.8, in Davis, *The Works of Plato* (1849) 2:214–15
[304] Plato, *The Republic* 3.11, in Davis, *The Works of Plato* (1849) 2:82

When he discovered that the square of the hypotenuse of every right-angled triangle is equal to the sum of the square of the two other sides, he did not sacrifice a hecatomb of cattle because he had discovered a mathematical but because he had discovered a law which Omnipotence had not enacted and could not repeal. The Deity, united in different quantities, but the proportion of the one to the other is either uniform, or some multiple were so-multiple of the former, by a number seldom very large. The same law prevails through the whole range of elements, and the proportions in which all combine with each other is expressed by a series of numbers.

> In every mineral species, there is a certain form of crystal, with axes intersecting at fixed angles, and bearing to each other definite proportions, from which, as a primary, every other form of crystal observed in that mineral species may be deduced, simply by varying the proportions of these axes. It is founded in each species the axes intersect each other at angles which are constant, and that the angles formed by the intersection of the phases are also related to each other according to certain definite laws.... Laws which nature seems to observe in the formation of mineral bodies.[305]

Everywhere in astronomy, numbers under proportions governed with unchanging permanency, a striking instance of which is the law of the inverse square of the distance, by which gravitation is governed, i.e. "that every particle of matter in the universe attracts every other particle, with a force varying inversely as the square of their mutual distances, and directly as the mass of the attracting particle."[306]

The leaves and flowers and the bones of animals are governed by like arithmetical laws, the same numbers controlling these and the suns and worlds of the universe.[307]

---

[305] James Nichol, *Manual of Mineralogy; or, the Natural History of the Mineral Kingdom*, [etc.] (Edinburgh: Adam and Charles Black, 1849), 6, 7

[306] Robert Grant, *History of Physical Astronomy, from the Earliest ages to the Middle of the XIXth Century: Comprehending a Detailed Account of the Establishment of the Theory of Gravitation by Newton, and its Development by his Successors; with an Exposition of the Progress of Research on all the Other Subjects of Celestial Physics* (London: Henry G. Bohn, 1852), 26

[307] For two insightful works on sacred geometry and numbers in nature, see Michael S. Sneider, *A Beginner's Guide to Constructing the Universe: Mathematical Archetypes of Nature, Art, and Science* (New York: HarperPerrenial, 1995), and John Michell, *How the World is Made:*

Numbers, abstractly considered, and disconnected from all object, cannot be conceived of by us as entities; or color, as disconnected with anything colored. So it is with form, and yet, "An analysis of objects into Matter and Form, when metaphorically extended from visible objects to things conceived in the most general manner, became an habitual hypothesis of the Aristotelian school";[308] and "Kant says that space and time are the forms of sensation."[309] Numbers are no more unreal then the Good, the Beautiful and the Perfect of Plato.[310]

Numbers are applicable to moral notions, to emotions and feelings, and their objects, as well as to the things of the material world. If numbers and their relations and proportions have always been intellectually concerned of by the deity, they have always been as real as form and ideas. And we cannot conceive that they were ever not present with the deity, or all the laws of mathematics not determined by him, unless we conceive of him as having been, before creation, and during an eternity, not only simple unity, no other unity co-existing with him, not even space or time, he himself the one at all, both subject and object; but unless we conceive of him as then been without thought, power, energy or act. The laws of numerical proportion were coexistent with the deity; and mathematical laws and relations governed in the creation of the universe. In the words of Professor Whewell, "the laws of the physical universe are resolvable into numerical relations, and therefore capable of being represented by mathematical formula."[311] And the mathematical doctrines of Plato, as he says, are put forward by him, "not so much as assertions concerning physical facts, of which the truth or falsehood is to be determined by a reference to nature herself, but as example of a truth of a higher kind than any reference to observation can give or contest, and as revelations of principles such as must have prevailed in the mind of the creator of the universe."[312] ... "These mathematical proportions are represented as realities more real than the phenomena;—as a natural philosophy of a higher kind

---

The Story of Creation According to Sacred Geometry 2d ed. (Rochester, Vermont: Inner Traditions, 2012)

[308] Whewell, *History of the Inductive Sciences* 3d ed. (1857), 1:42

[309] Whewell, *History of the Inductive Sciences* 3d ed. (1857), 1:42

[310] For a work on the transcendentals contemporary with Pike, see O.W. Wight, trans., M.V. Cousin, *The True, the Beautiful and the Good* (New York: D. Appleton and Co., 1879)

[311] Whewell, *History of the Inductive Sciences* 3d ed. (1857), 1:348. Whewell credits "Professor Thomson (A. Butler's *Lectures*, Third Series, Lect. i. Note 11.)." For the reference, see William Hepworth Thompson, ed., William Archer Butler, *Lectures on the History of Ancient Philosophy* 2 vols. (Cambridge: Macmillan and Co., 1856) 2:171 fnt. 11

[312] Whewell, *History of the Inductive Sciences* 3d ed. (1857), 1:351

than the study of nature itself can teach. This is no doubt an erroneous assumption: yet even in this there is a grain of truth, namely, that the mathematical laws which prevail in the universe, involve mathematical truths, which, being demonstrated of, or of a higher and more cogent kind than mere experimental truths."[313]

Doctor Whewell says, that "the relations of space and number are the alphabet in which the laws of nature are written,"[314] and that "there exist respecting number, many truths absolutely necessary, entirely independent of experience, and anterior to it."[315]... "The universality and necessity which distinguish them can by no means be derived from experience. These characters do in reality flow from the ideas which these truths involve, and when the necessity of truth is exhibited in the way of logic: demonstration, it is found to depend upon certain fundamental principles (definitions and axioms), which may thus be considered as expressing, in some measure, the essential characters of an idea)."[316]... "Necessary truths must be universal truths. If any property belongs to a right angled triangle *necessarily*, it must belong to *all* right-angled triangles."[317]

If there had never been a right-angled triangle, a circle or a figure with four sides, it would be nonetheless absolutely true, that whenever there should be a right-angled triangle, the sum of the squares of the number of equal parts of the base and perpendicular would equal the square of the number of like equal parts of the hypotenuse: it would be equally true that the radius of any circle whatever would be equal to each side of a hexagon inscribed in the circle; and that the tangent of any one of any circle would be equal to the radius multiplied by the sine divided by the cosine of the same arc; and it would be equally true that the sum of the angles of any figure of four sides would be equal to four right angles, as the sum of the angles of a triangle would be equal to two right angles.

We cannot conceive that these truths, in any other of the *necessary* truths in regard to numbers, can depend upon any, even a Supreme Will, for their existence. They are truths that must always have existed in the Divine Intellect.

---

[313] Whewell, *History of the Inductive Sciences* 3d ed. (1857), 1:351

[314] William Whewell, *History of Scientific Ideas Being the First Part of the Philosophy of the Inductive Sciences* 3d ed. 2 vols. (London: John Parker and Son, 1858), 1:105

[315] Whewell, *History of Scientific Ideas* (1858) 1:132

[316] Whewell, *History of Scientific Ideas* (1858) 1:58

[317] Whewell, *History of Scientific Ideas* (1858) 1:64

"There is a definite relation between the notes of stings and forces which stretch them; and this truth is the ground-work of the theory of musical concords and discords."[318] "The rate of vibration of a string, on which its note depends, is, other things being equal, [not as the weight, but] as the square root of the weight"[319] that stretches it. "And the ratios of 2 to 1, 3 to 2, and 4 to 3 are the characteristic ratios of the octave, fifth and fourth.... The proportion in major third is 5 to 4; in a minor third, 6 to 5.... These and other arithmetical elements of music are important and fundamental portions of the Science of Harmonics."[320]

Doctor Whewell says that though Plato's "notion of a real intelligible world, of which the visible world was a fleeting and changeable shadow, was extravagant, yet it led him to seek to determine the forms of the intelligible things, which are really the laws of visible phenomena"[321] and that his ideas, "so far as they were they the intelligible forms of visible things, were really fit objects of philosophical research."[322] And he adds, that if ideas cannot be the causes or principles of things, they may be and must be, the conditions and principles of our knowledge which is what we want them to be.[323]

As the thought of God creates, and all the future has always been now, to Him, the intelligible idea of the universe formed by and within Him, was real, and also the cause and principle of the created universe, if thought is real and if the Divine Thought is, when uttered, the visible creation. Even in the case of a human inventor, his hands only embody in matter the plan and idea formed in his mind; and if the idea could be so embodied or, rather, expressed by a mere exertion of the will, sure the convention could be said to exist in idea, before its expression, as a word or sentence does, before it is uttered.

The Divine conceptions of number are as much laws of visible phenomena, as the forms of intelligible things are; for these forms are fixed and determined, in part, at least, by numbers; and numbers also, as well as forms, are the conditions and principles of our knowledge.

I have spoken incidentally of flowers is also subject to the laws of numbers. "Some flowers consist of three or five equal sets of organs,

---

[318] Whewell, *History of Scientific Ideas* (1858) 1:82

[319] Whewell, *History of Scientific Ideas* (1858) 1:83; Pike accidently omitted the bracketed words.

[320] Whewell, *History of Scientific Ideas* (1858) 1:83

[321] William Whewell, *On the Philosophy of Discovery, Chapters Historical and Critical; Including the Completion of the Third Edition of the Philosophy of the Inductive Sciences* (London: John W. Parker and Son, 1860), 29

[322] Whewell, *On the Philosophy of Discovery* (1860), 29

[323] Whewell, *On the Philosophy of Discovery* (1860), 29–30

similarly and regularly disposed, as the iris has *three* straight petals, and three reflexed ones, alternately dispersed, [and] the rose has *five* equal and similar sepals of the calyx, and alternate with these, as many petals of the corolla."[324] The triangular symmetry "occur[s] in a large class of flowers, as, for example, in all the lily tribe,"[325] and is found also in crystals. "The pentagonal symmetry ... occurs abundantly in the vegetable world, but never among crystals,"[326] and does not appear to be a possible form there.

The square or to tetragonal symmetry occurs in crystals abundantly, but appears to be less congenial to the vegetable world, and the deviation from the usual type of vegetable forms. The trigonal or three-membered symmetry occurs abundantly both in plants and crystals. The pentagonal form appears in the animal kingdom, but the trigonal and tetragonal do not.[327]

Doctor Whewell, *History of Scientific Ideas*, from whom I take these facts, says:

> The regular, or as they may be called, the *normal* types of the vegetable world appear to be the forms which possess triangular and pentagonal symmetry; from these the others may be conceived to be derived, by transformations resulting from the expansion of one or more parts.... [T]hese various kinds of symmetry include relations both of form and of number, but more especially of the latter kind; and as this symmetry is often an important character in various classes of natural objects, such classes have often curious numerical properties. One of the most remarkable and extensive of these is the distinction which prevails between monocotyledonous and dicotyledonous plants; the number *three* being the ground of the symmetry of the former, and the number *five*, of the latter. Thus liliaceous and bulbous plants, and the like, have flowers of three or six petals, and the other organs follow the same numbers: while the vast majority of plants are pentandrous, and with their five stamens have also their other parts in fives. This great numerical

---

[324] Whewell, *History of Scientific Ideas* (1858) 2:68
[325] Whewell, *History of Scientific Ideas* (1858) 2:69
[326] Whewell, *History of Scientific Ideas* (1858) 2:69
[327] Whewell, *History of Scientific Ideas* (1858) 2:70

distinction corresponding to a leading difference of physiological structure cannot but be considered as a highly curious fact in phytology. Such properties of numbers, thus connected in an incomprehensible manner with fundamental and extensive laws of nature, give to numbers an appearance of mysterious importance and efficacy. We learn from history how strongly the study of such properties, as they are exhibited by the phenomena of the heavens, took possession of the mind of Kepler; perhaps it was this which, at an earlier period, contributed in no small degree to the numerical mysticism of the Pythagoreans in antiquity, and of the Arabians and others in the middle ages. In crystallography, numbers are the primary characters in which the properties of substances are expressed; they appear, first, in that classification of forms which depends on the degree of symmetry, that is, upon the number of correspondences; and next, in the laws of derivation, which, for the most part, appear to be common in their occurrence in proportion to the numerical simplicity of their expression. But the manifestation of a governing numerical relation in the organic world strikes us as more unexpected; and the selection of the number *five* as the index of the symmetry of dicotyledonous plants and radiated animals, (a number which is nowhere symmetrically produced in inorganic bodies,) makes this a new and remarkable illustration of the constancy of numerical relations.[328]

Artedi and Linnaeus found the number of rays in the membrane of the gills, and the number of rays in the fins, a fish, to be important elements in its ichthyological classification.[329]

If Pythagoras had known these curious facts, discovered by modern science, how much more reason would he have had to say "numbers and music by the principles of the entire universe, and the world is regulated by numerical harmony."

---

[328] Whewell, *History of Scientific Ideas* (1858) 2:70–72

[329] William Whewell, *History of the Inductive Sciences, from the Earliest to the Present Time* 2 vols. (New York: D. Appleton and Co., 1858), 2:424

The same obedience to numbers appears in the distances of the planets from the sun. In the last century, Professor Bode discovered the construction of a regular series of numbers, in coincidence with which the distances of all the known planets from the sun and been arranged by their Creator, saving one exception.[330]

Representing the distance of Mercury from the Sun by four, Venus is distance represented by seven, and the Earth by 10. These distances increase in an arithmetical ratio; but those of the other planets in Greece in a geometrical ratio thus:

Earth,   10
Mars,   16, the increase being   6
Jupiter, 52,   ”   ”   ”   12 + 24 = 36
Saturn, 100, ”   ”   ”   48

The one of the regular number between Mars and Jupiter, and the discovery of Ceres and Pallas led to the calculation that there had originally been a planet between Mars and Jupiter,[331] with the distance from the sun represented by 28, and that it had been broken up into asteroids.

It is been found that the distance of Uranus and Neptune agree with this law, and are represented by 196 and 388. Thus each increase of distance is double the preceding increase, from Mars to Neptune, these increments been represented by 6, 12, 24, 36, 48, 96, 192.

Another formula of these is:

Mercury	4
Venus	$4 + 3 \cdot 2^0$
Terra	$4 + 3 \cdot 2^1$
Mars	$4 + 3 \cdot 2^2$
Ceres	$4 + 3 \cdot 2^3$
Jupiter	$4 + 3 \cdot 2^4$

---

[330] Bode's law (aka the Titius-Bode law) provides the approximate distances of planets from the Sun. It suggests that each planet should be about twice the distance from the sun as the preceding one. Although it anticipated the orbits of Ceres (in the asteroid belt) and Uranus, it fails to accurately account for planets beyond Pluto.

[331] This was the prevailing theory in Pike's day. Today it is believed that the asteroid belt is the residue of protoplanets which, under Jupiter's tremendous gravity, collided with too much force to coalesce into a planet.

Saturn	$4 + 3 \cdot 2^5$
Uranus	$4 + 3 \cdot 2^6$
Neptune	$4 + 3 \cdot 2^7$

Bode's Law being, "if we represent the distance of Mercury by four, in inquiries following terms by the product of three into the ascending powers of two, we shall obtain the relative distances of the planets from the sun."

Kepler's third law, in relation to the revolutions of the planets is another striking instance. It is, that the squares. Times of revolution are in constant ratio to the cubes of the major accidents of their orbits. And another lot is, that the masses of the planets are as one cube of the distances from the sun, divided by the squares of the period times.

7, Sayce says, "was a sacred number [which came] to the Semites from their Accadian predecessors.... Seven by seven the magic knots had to be tied by the witch; seven times the body of the sick man to be anointed with purifying oil.... 'The God of the number seven' received particular honor."[332] "The deluge was said to have lasted 7 days. Three groups of stars, the *tikpi* (or circles?), the *masi* or 'double stars' and the *lumasi* or 'sheep of the hero,' where each seven in number. The gates which led to Hades were 7; Erech was the city of 'the seven zones' or 'stones.' ... [The] prayer [was to be made] 7 times over the thread."[333]

---

[332] A[rchibald]. H[enry]. Sayce, *Lectures on the Origin and Growth of Religion: As Illustrated by the Religion of the Ancient Babylonians* (London: Williams and Norgate, 1887), 82

[333] Sayce, *Lectures on the Origin and Growth of Religion* (1887), 82 fnt. 2a

APPENDIX[334]

THE *DE ISIDE ET OSIRIDE* OF PLUTARCH

The Glory of God is to Conceal the Word:
and Wisdom is with those who keep Secrets.

PLUTARCH, author of the treatise *De Iside et Osiride*, as it is usually called, it being in Greek, and its title Περὶ Ἴσιδος καὶ Ὀσίριδος, was born, it is supposed, A.D. 46. He was the Preceptor of Trajan, afterward Emperor, A.D. 76, and Governor of Illyricum under Trajan, A.D. 105. Iamblichus flourished two hundred and fifty years later, about 300–320 A.D., in the time of Constantine the Great.

Pythagoras flourished six hundred years and more before Plutarch, and eight hundred and seven before Iamblichos, about 550 years B.C. Cyrus conquered Babylonia 538 B.C.; and Plato was born 429 B.C.

It may be at once said, that when Plutarch wrote, nothing was known of the ancient history of Egypt, or of the ancient doctrines or Deities of the Egyptians, with any degree of accuracy; and that what has been written as to the celebration of Mysteries in Ancient Egypt, as well as elsewhere, is for the most part sheer fiction.

So, too, it may be at once said, that in the time even of Plutarch, the explanations which Pythagoras possessed, and except from a few concealed, of the Symbols which he used, had been utterly lost. Nothing was known to the writers of the time of Trajan, of the sacred books or doctrines of the Indo-Aryans or the Irano-Aryans, or of the Sanskrit or Zend languages, both long before dead.

BRYANT says, in his "Analysis of Antient Mythology" (i. 180): "The Isis and Osiris of PLUTARCH may be admitted with proper circumspection. It may be said that the whole is still an enigma: and I must confess that it is: but we receive it more copiously exemplified, and more clearly defined; and it must necessarily be more genuine, by being nearer the fountain-head; so that by comparing; and adjusting The various parts, we are more likely to arrive at a solution of the hidden purport."

One who carefully studies this enigma, this work of Plutarch, *De Iside et Osiride*, will be struck with many glimpses which it intentionally, and yet in appearance accidentally gives us of the inner secrets of the ancient mysteries; and with the light which it throws upon the

---

[334] Extracted from Albert Pike, *Readings XXXII* (ca. 1880)

obscurest parts of Masonry. It is as though the wind lifted a corner of the impenetrable veil, at intervals, and only for a moment, with which the art and jealousy of the old Hierophants have carefully hidden from the eyes of all of us the esoteric meaning of the Words and Symbols of the Royal and Sacerdotal art.

According to Iamblichos, PLUTARCH declared that it was in the Mysteries of Orpheus, celebrated in Thrace, he had learned the unity of the First and Final Cause; or, to make use of his symbolic expressions, he had learned that "the Eternal Substance of Number was the Intelligent Principle of the Universe, of the Heavens, of the earth, and of mixed beings." —*Life of Pythagoras, sec.* 146.

The Mysteries were in fact not established to teach the unity of a God, and the doctrines of Creation, Providence, and a life to come; but to transmit those great truths, which had been recognized in all times, and had been uttered in the most ancient spoken words. —*Court de Gebelin*, iv. 317.

Stobæus has preserved in his dictionary a passage from an ancient author, which paints in a very vivid manner the startling spectacle of the Initiations.

"The Soul," says this author, "experiences at death the same emotions as it feels during initiation; and even the terms respond to each other as the realities do: *To die*, and *to be initiated* being expressed by words almost the same." [*Teleutan* and *Teleisthai*, both derived from *tel*, end. *Death* is the end of animal life; *Initiation* is the *end* of profane life, the death of vice.] "At first, there is nothing but errors and uncertainties, laborious journeys, toilsome and terrific circuits through the thick darkness of night. Arrived at the confines of death and initiation, everything presents itself under a terrible aspect; all is horror, trepidation, dread, alarm. But when these terrifying objects have passed, a miraculous and divine light strikes the eyes, brilliant plains and meadows enameled with flowers are everywhere discovered, and hymns and musical choruses enchant the ears. The sublime doctrines of *The Holy Science* are the subject of conversation. Sacred and awe-inspiring visions wrap the senses in admiration. Initiated and made perfect, one is afterward free, is no longer subjected to any restraint. Crowned and triumphant, one walks through the regions of the Blessed, converses with holy and virtuous men, and the Sacred Mysteries are celebrated to the utmost of his desire." Such was what was then called Palingenesis, Regeneration, the New Birth. (*Court de Gebelin*, iv. 321)

Eusebius and Clement of Alexandria give a fragment of one of those Hymns that were sung at the opening of the Mysteries, and which gives a grand idea of them.

"I am about," said the Hierophant, "I am about to make known a secret to the Initiates. Let the entrances to these places be closed against the Profane! O, Musæus thou who didst descend from the brilliant Selēnē hear my words! I will announce to thee important truths. Permit not prejudices and prepossessions to deprive thee of the happiness which thou desirest to find in the knowledge of the mysterious truths. Consider Divine Nature; incessantly contemplate her; keep thy mind and heart ever right; and advancing along a safe path, admire the Master of the Universe! He is ONE, Self-Existent; to him all Beings owe their being. He acts in all things and everywhere. Invisible to the eyes of mortals, He Himself sees all things." (*Court de Gebelin*, iv. 323)

"Initiated, and made Perfect, one is afterward Free." Hence it is that in the Ancient and Accepted Rite, we call ourselves "Perfect Freemasons"; that we see the Dead raised; and undergo those tests and trials that are the symbols of those by means of which, according to the ancient faith, the soul was made fit to ascend through the seven spheres to its primal home.

Of this initiation Plutarch enigmatically writes; and it will perhaps not be unprofitable to occupy a little while in endeavoring to extract the meaning of his mystic utterances. The Sphinx, silent and mysterious, was the apt symbol of the old Hierophant; and Plutarch, was one of the Initiated.

"To desire and covet after Truth, those Truths, more especially, which respect the Divine Nature, is to aspire to be partakers of that Nature itself, and to profess that all our studies and inquiries are devoted to the acquisition of holiness; an employment surely more truly religious than any external purifications or mere service of the temple can be ... Isis, according to the Greek interpretation of the word, signifies *Knowledge*; as the name of her professed adversary *Tūpho* means *Insolence* and *Pride*; a name therefore extremely well adapted to one, who full of ignorance and error, tears in pieces and conceals that Holy Doctrine which the goddess collects, compiles, and delivers to those who aspire after the most perfect participation of the Divine Nature; a *Doctrine* which, by commanding a steady perseverance in one uniform and temperate course of life, and an abstinence from particular kinds of food, as well as from all indulgence in venery, restrains the intemperate and voluptuous part within bounds, and at the same time habituates her votaries to undergo those austere and rigid ceremonies which their religion obliges them to observe. The end of all which is, that by these means they may be the better prepared *for the attainment of the Knowledge of the First and Supreme Mind*, whom the Goddess exhorts them to search after, as dwelling near and constantly residing with her. For this reason, her Temple, in the same language, is called Iseion *alluding to that knowledge of the Eternal and Self-existent Being, which may be there obtained*, if it be properly approached, *with due purity and sanctity of manners.*" (Plutarch, *de Iside et Osiride*, 2)

"Isis … being none other, as it is said, than Wisdom pointing out the knowledge of divine truths to her votaries, the true *Hierophoroi* and *Hierostoloi*. Now, by the former of these are meant, *such who carry about them locked up in their souls as in a chest, the sacred doctrine concerning the Gods*, purified from all such superfluities as superstition may have annexed to it; whilst the holy habit, with which the latter of them adorn the Statues of the Deities, partly of a dark and gloomy, and partly of a more bright and shining color, seems aptly enough to represent the notions which this doctrine teaches us to entertain of the Divine

Nature itself, partly clear and partly obscure. And forasmuch as the devotees of Isis after their decease are wrapped up in these sacred vestments, is not this intended to signify, *that this* Holy Doctrine *still abides with them*, and that this alone accompanies them in another life? … He alone is a true servant or follower of this Goddess, who after he has heard, and been made acquainted in a proper manner with the history of the actions of these Gods, searches into the hidden truths which lie, concealed under them, and examines the whole by the dictates of Reason and Philosophy." (ibid., 3)

To desire and covet after Truth, and especially after those truths that respect the Divine Nature; this is the object of Masonry; which is, as we learn at our initiation into the first degree of the lesser or popular mysteries, a *Search after Light*; after Light, which, we are soon taught to understand, is Truth, "a Divine attribute and the basis of every virtue." In search of this Truth, which is light, that is, the very substance of the Omnipresent God, the אור the Aor, or *Essence of Light*, the pure *Ether* of which the material or physical light is but the out-shining and manifestation—in search of this, we continually advance toward the East; as Pythagoras and many other of the early sages repaired to the Great Orient in search of philosophical Truth; of that knowledge of the Divine Nature, to aspire to which "is to aspire to be partakers of that

Nature itself." In the highest degrees we profess to be, and we hope we are, in the Grand Orient, the very home and shrine of all the Truth in regard to the Divine Nature, of which man can be in possession.

As with the Ancient *Hierophoroi*, "who carried about them *locked up in their souls, as in a chest*"—as in *the Ark of the Covenant*, hidden in the Soul's depths, *beneath the nine arches*, "the Sacred Doctrine," the *ἱερος λόγος*, concerning the Gods, so with true Masons, all their studies and inquiries are devoted to the acquisition of *Holiness*, "an employment more truly religious than any external purifications or mere service of the Temple can be." *Holiness*, alluded to in lower degrees, where the *Sanctum Sanctorum*, or Holy of Holies, is spoken of [קֹדֶש־הַקֳּדָשִׁים בֵּית, *Bith Kadosh h'Kadoshim*], of the Temple built by Solomon, is that to which the 30th Degree of the Ancient and Accepted Rite is peculiarly devoted.

The especial characteristics, Plutarch says, of the goddess Isis, are *Wisdom* and *Philosophy*. Her name in the Greek, derived from *ἴσκω* or *εἴδω* or *ἴσημι*, *video*, I *see* or *know*, means *knowledge, Wisdom*, the second Sephirah of the Hebrews, the חכמה , *Hakemah* or *Hokmah*, of the Kabbalah.

The object of Masons, like that of the aspirants "after the most perfect participation of the Divine Nature," to whom Isis delivers the *ἱερòν λόγον*, the Holy Doctrine is, "that by these means they may be the better prepared for the attainment of the knowledge [*γνοσις, Gnõsis*] of the First, the Lordly, the cognizable by the intellect only" [*τοῦ πρώτου καὶ κυρίου καὶ νοητοῦ*] the knowledge and cognizance of *The Being* [*τοῦ ὄντος*], that is, of the Very Deity, Ahura Mazda.

Isis [*Initiation*] is Dikaiosūnē, also; *Righteousness* or *Justice*; and *Wisdom, Sophia, Hakemah*, "pointing out the knowledge of divine things to her votaries." She is the daughter of Hermes [Khurm, Hiram, or Huram], or of Prometheus; of whom the former is said to have communicated to men the knowledge of Grammar [or Letters], and Music; and the latter to have given them the inestimable boon of Fire [Light or Truth], or, as Plutarch says, of Wisdom and Foresight [*Pronoia*, Prudence].

The clothing of the images of the Gods, part black, and part white, symbolical of the Duality of the Divine Nature, is imitated in the clothing of the Kadosh, white bordered with black, and the hilt of his dagger, half ivory, half ebony. In this mystery of Good and Evil we find the Beneficent Mind or Divine Wisdom, and the Malign Mind, its opposite and antagonist, of the creed of Zarathustra; and the investiture of the

Isiacs[335] after their death in these two colors, is a symbol showing that this Logos [*Word* or *Doctrine*], "still abides with them, and that it alone accompanies them in another life." This *"True and Ineffable Word"* of the Perfect Elu, the meaning of which is the Royal Secret, is that by means of which the Adepts were enabled to travel into far countries and there to receive the wages of a Master.

And he alone is a *Master* Mason, or true Follower of Isis, "who searches into the hidden truths that lie concealed" under the commonplace interpretations of the legend and symbols of the third degree, "and examines the whole by the dictates of Reason and Philosophy."

"Nor, indeed, ought such an examination to be looked upon as unnecessary, whilst so many persons are ignorant of the true reason even of the most ordinary rites observed by the Egyptian Priests.... Some, indeed, there are, *who never trouble themselves to think at all about these matters; whilst others rest satisfied with the most superficial accounts of them.*" (ibid. 4)

As most Masons do with what are called the *explanations* of the ceremonies and symbols of Masonry; as, for example, with those of the candidate being "neither barefoot nor shod"; of his being deprived "of all metallic substances"; of the female at the broken column, with "Time combing out the ringlets of her hair"; of "chalk, charcoal, and clay"; of one and then both points of the *compasses* being raised above the *square*; of the reason for investiture with the "cable-tow"; and many other of our ceremonies and symbols.

"When we are told by *Hesiod*, 'not to pare our nails, whilst we are present at the festivals of the Gods,' we ought so to understand him, as if he designed thereby to inculcate that purity with which we ought to come prepared, before we enter 'upon any religious duty, that we have not to make ourselves clean, whilst we ought to be occupied in attending to the solemnity itself." (ibid., 4)

Q. Where were you first prepared to be a Mason?
A. In my heart.

---

[335] Isiacs were followers of the Egyptian goddess Isis, the sister-wife of Osiris, whom she revived in order to bear his child (Horus). During the Hellenistic period, under the influence of Ptolemy, a type of syncretism altered the nature of some of the Egyptian gods, including Isis, who had several roles, including one similar to the Virgin Mary. Her worship, which included secrets rites, spread to Rome and became a challenge to the traditional Roman gods. It gradually gained acceptance, and even support, remaining popular until the early Fourth Century, when Constantine converted to Christianity.

And the naked foot, knee, and breast, make personal cleanliness, the symbol, most natural and obvious, of purity of the Soul, indispensable.

"The religious rites and ceremonies of the Egyptians were never instituted upon irrational grounds, never built upon mere fable and superstition, but founded with a view to promote the morality and happiness of those who were to observe them; or at least to preserve the memory of some valuable piece of history, *or to represent to us some of the phenomena of nature.*" (ibid., 8)

"The kings of Egypt were always taken from amongst either the Soldiery or the Priests…. If the choice fell upon a Soldier, he was immediately initiated into the Order of Priests, and by them instructed in their abstruse and hidden philosophy—a philosophy for the most part enwrapped in myths and parables, and exhibiting only dark hints and obscure resemblances of the Truth. And thus much even the Priests themselves hint to us in many instances, particularly in those Sphinxes which they seem designedly to have placed before their Temples, as types of the enigmatical nature of their Theology. To this purpose likewise is that inscription which they have engraved upon the base of the statue of Minerva [*Athena*] (whom also they call *Isis*) at Sais; '*I am all that has become, that Is, and shall be; and no mortal has ever discovered what my veil conceals.*' In like manner the word *Amoun* [or, in Greek, *Ammōn*], which is generally regarded as the proper name of the Egyptian Jupiter, is interpreted by Manetho the Sebennite, to signify *the hidden*, and concealment … their invoking Amoun is the same thing as calling on the Supreme Being, whom they suppose invisible and concealed in the universal Nature, to appear and manifest Himself to them. So cautious and reserved was the Egyptian Wisdom in those things that appertain to religion." (ibid., 9)

It is or seems to be the general notion, that the symbols of *Masonry* are used and were appropriated or invented as explanations; as a sort of picture-writing, intended to render easy the acquisition of knowledge. Hence the absurd, superficial and commonplace interpretations of them, that make one wonder why they should have been used to express such trite, tame, and ordinary truths or lessons.

But the real fact is, that they were used to *conceal* the truth; as a means, not of teaching it to, but of *hiding it from*, the vulgar. It was never meant that they should be easily interpreted. Like the symbols of the Egyptian Hierophants, every one is a Sphinx (half buried in the sand, moreover,) that only an Œdipus can interpret. The consequence is, that the ordinary interpretations of our symbols and ceremonies are simply absurd.

"None of the Grecian Philosophers seem to having paid a more especial regard to the method of philosophizing of the Priests, than Pythagoras, who has particularly imitated their mysterious and symbolical manner [τὸ συμβολικὸν καὶ μυστηριῶδες] in his own writings, and like them conveyed his doctrines to the world in enigmas. For many of the Pythagoric precepts come nothing short of the hieroglyphical representations themselves.

"It is my opinion, that when the Pythagoreans appropriate the names of several of the gods to particular number as that of *Apollo* to the *Unit*, of *Diana* to the *Duad*, of *Minerva* to *Seven*, and of *Neptune* to *the first cube* (8), *in this they allude to something which the Founder of their Sect saw in the Egyptian Temples, to some ceremonies performed in them, or to some symbols there exhibited.*" (ibid. 10)

Plutarch supposed that Pythagoras brought his Symbols from Egypt, and concealed in them the religious and mystical notions of the Egyptians. But they are not Egyptian Symbols, nor can they be interpreted by the Egyptian doctrines. They came from the Median Magi.

The Sun and the Moon are two lights of the Lodge. *Why* they are so, Masons are not now told. They learn, indeed, that these are associated with the Master of the Lodge, another of its Lights, and that the latter is one of the three because it is his business to dispense light there, as the Sun gives light by day and the Moon by night.

The Sun has always been the Symbol of the Generative power. In the Khordah-Avesta, a work of a later age than that of Zarathustra, but much earlier than the Conquest of Babylonia by the Medes and Persians, Maonh, in modern Persian, Mah, the Moon, is female, and is praised in the Mah-Yasht as the producer of cattle and of vegetation, as bringing greenness, fruits, and health. She was the Symbol of the productive Capacity of Nature. In Egypt, the Sun and Moon represented Osiris and Isis.

"*A Heart placed in the midst of a flaming censer* is made use of by the Egyptians to characterize the Heavens; which by reason of their being eternal, never are consumed or wax old.... For can it be imagined that it is the dog himself that is thus reverenced by them under the name of Hermes? They are the qualities of this animal, his constant vigilance, and his acumen in distinguishing his friends from his foes, which have rendered him, as Plato expresses it, a fit emblem of that God who is the more immediate patron of Reason....

"If you, therefore, in this manner, O *Clea*, hear and entertain the story of these Gods, from those who know how to explain it consistently with religion and philosophy, if you will steadfastly continue in the performance of all those Holy Rites which the laws require of you, and are moreover fully persuaded that to possess correct opinions in regard to the Gods is more acceptable to them than any sacrifice or mere external act of worship can be, you will thereby be exempt from any danger of falling into Superstition; an evil no les to be avoided than Atheism itself. (ibid., 11)

So if a Mason hears and entertains the myth (*ὁ μῦθος*) of the third degree, from those who know how to expound it in accordance with piety and philosophy; and if he at all times observes all the Holy Rites that are prescribed, and seeks, by forming true ideas of the Divine Nature, to find for himself "The True Word," his progress in Masonry will indeed be an advance toward The Light. The blazing or flaming heart, in the emblazonry of the 32d degree, is an apt emblem of incombustibility, and therefore of immortality.

Isis, "after much pains and difficulty, by means of some *dogs* that conducted her to the place where it was," found *Anubis*, her sister's child, and bred it up. In the ninth degree, a dog is the means of discovering the hiding place of the chief of the assassins.

"There are other circumstances in the Egyptian ritual, which hint to us the reality upon which this history is grounded, such as their cleaving the trunk of a tree, their wrapping it up in linen, which they tear to pieces for that purpose, and the libations of oil which they afterward pour upon it; but these I do not insist upon, *because they are intermixed with such of their mysteries as may not be revealed.*" (ibid., 21)

"The like may be affirmed also *of those other things which are so carefully concealed from the vulgar under the cover of mysteries and initiations.*" (ibid., 2)

"It is from these things [the senseless and inanimate], that we learn the true nature of the Gods, that they are not different amongst different people, that they are not some of them peculiar to the Greeks, and others to the Barbarians, some of them northern and others southern Deities; but that as the sun and moon, and the heavens and the earth and the sea, though common to all mankind, have different names given them by different people; so may the same likewise be affirmed of that

One Supreme Reason who framed tins world, and of that One Providence which governs and watches over the whole, and of those subordinate ministering Powers that are set over the Universe; that they are the very same everywhere, though the honors which are paid them, as well as the appellations given them, are different in different places according to the laws of each country; as are likewise those symbols, *under which the Mystics endeavor to lead their votaries to the knowledge of Divine Truths*; and though some of these are more clear and explicit than others, *yet are they not any of them without hazard*; for whilst some persons, by wholly mistaking their meaning and application, have plunged into Superstition, others, to avoid so fatal a quagmire, have unawares dashed themselves against the rock of Atheism." (ibid., 67)

"SERAPIS is none other than that common name by which all those are called *who have thus changed their nature*" [as Osiris did when translated from the order of Genii to that of Gods]; "*as is well known by those who are initiated into the Mysteries of Osiris.*" (ibid., 28)

"Time begets all things out of itself, bearing them with itself, as it were in a womb; *but this is one of those secret doctrines which are more fully made known to those who are initiated into the worship of Anubis.*" (ibid., 34)

"Nor is it Osiris's dead body only, but those likewise of the other Gods, as many of them as had a beginning and consequently were corruptible, which, *the Priests tell us, were after their deaths deposited with them, and carefully preserved, whilst their souls were translated to Heaven, there to shine forth in so many stars*. Thus, in particular, was the Soul of Isis translated into what the Greeks call the *dog-star* and the Egyptians, *Sothis*, Horus's into Orion, and Typhon's into the Bear." (ibid., 21)

"Isis herself, some say, in memory of the great contests and difficulties which she had undergone, and of the wanderings whereunto she had been exposed, unwilling likewise that so much courage and resolution as upon this occasion had been displayed, should be lost in perpetual silence, *appointed certain Rites and Mysteries*, which were to be as images, representations, or imitations rather of what was then done and suffered; with this further view likewise, that the commemoration of these events might serve as incitements to piety, and as a proper consolation to all those, whether men or women, who might at any time after be in like circumstances of distress." (ibid., 34)

"So again, the histories upon which the most solemn feasts of Bacchus, the *Titania* and *Nuktelia* are founded, do they not exactly correspond with what we are told of the cutting in pieces of Osiris, of his rising again, and of his new life? nor does what relates to his burial in any way contradict this notion." (ibid., 35)

"The word *Amoun* is interpreted by Manetho the Sebennite to signify concealment, or something which is *hidden*. Hecataus of Abdera indeed tells us, that the Egyptians make use of this term when they call out to one another; and if so, then their invoking *Amoun* is the same thing as calling upon the Supreme Being (*whom they suppose hidden and concealed in the Universal Nature*) to appear and manifest itself to them." (ibid., 9)

*   *   *   *   *   *

"They further add that Isis and Osiris, having a mutual affection, enjoyed each other in their mother's womb, before they were born, and that from this commerce sprang *Aroueris*, whom the Egyptians likewise call the elder *Horus* and the Greeks *Apollo*." (ibid., 12)

"The Egyptians are wont to give Horus the name of Kaimis, by which word they mean 'Something which may be seen'; for this world is perceptible to the senses, and visible." (ibid., 56)

Plutarch was like a man walking in the dark. The "Something which may be seen" is that which is manifested or revealed, *i.e.*, the Divine Wisdom, Isis, manifesting itself as the Divine Word or Utterance, in Humanity—Vohu-Mano.

Isis, he says, was also called Muth (mother), Athyri (that in which Osiris *is*); and Methuer, Plenitude and Excellence. (ibid., 56)

She is to be considered, he says, as one who always participates of the Supreme God and is ever in conjunction with Him. That is, she is the Divine Wisdom, immanent in the Deity; the Deity in so far as he is Wisdom. (ibid., 53)

The delineations, forms and Emanations (out-flowings, manifestations, revealings) of the Deity are diffused, he says, throughout the Heavenly bodies. All these, the Vedic Poets said, are the self-manifestations of Indra, the Light. (ibid., 59)

Plato asserts, he says, that the old name by which the Ancients expressed the essence of things, was derived from a word of the same import with this of Isis: and then, to hide what he means, "that knowledge, wisdom, understanding, the chief-good, and even virtue itself had their names, in the Greek language, originally taken from this same, or a root of similar signification." (ibid., 60)

"Osiris is supposed to be that common reason, which pervades the superior and inferior regions of the universe—the universal reason, called by them Anubis, and sometimes likewise Hermanubis." (ibid., 61)

"Isis is frequently called by them *Athena*, signifying in their language, 'I proceeded from myself.' " (ibid., 62)

"The mind and reason of the Supreme God, which in its own nature is invisible to us, and dwelling in obscurity [hidden] by putting itself into motion proceeds to the production of other beings." (ibid., 62)

"Whatever beings are endued with life, with the faculty of seeing, that have a principle of voluntary motion in them, and that are able to distinguish what belongs to, and is proper for them, and what not, all these are to be regarded as the effluxes, as it were, or as so many portions taken off from that Supreme Providential Wisdom, that governs the universe." (ibid., 77)

It is evident, from these extracts, that the principal purpose of the Mysteries was to teach the Initiates "*the Secret or Holy Doctrine*," the Theology and Philosophy, which the Priests concealed from the vulgar, as beyond and above their comprehension. Plutarch, it is equally evident, was, like Herodotus, an Initiate; and could therefore give only glimpses of the truth, and hints understandable by the Initiates alone. To much of what he thus disclosed to them only, the key is now lost, but somewhat the well-informed and studious Mason can still understand.

French writers say that the antiquarian, ELIAS ASHMOLE, digested and arranged the myth and ceremonial of the Blue degrees. And if we found in Plutarch, or in any other work treating of the Ancient Mysteries, much that is literally reproduced in Masonry, it would be permissible to conclude that the coincidences exist, not because Masonry and those Mysteries are one, or parent and child, but because the modern compiler of Masonry borrowed these from the old ceremonial, in order to give his work the air and aspect of a venerable antiquity.

It is much more satisfactory evidence of identity, when the coincidences are not thus perfect, and when Masonry only draws aside a corner of the curtain that hides, and for many centuries has hidden, those grey and venerable mysteries; for else we should have to ignore and deny the wasting influences of time, and that the memory of ancient things fades away and becomes indistinct.

As in the long succession of generations words in the same language change, and one letter displaces another, until words no longer appear the same; as inflections vary, and particles appear or vanish and are disused, and yet the grammatical forms abundantly prove the identity of the ancient and modern tongues, when in the mere words one seems an alien to the other; so in Masonry, when all the details of the ceremonial have been changed, and even the symbols are no longer in important respects the same, and their present interpretations were never even dreamed of by the ancient Sages, still its identity with the ancient Mysteries is amply proven by the most satisfactory of all evidence, identity of objects, identity of doctrine, and substantial identity of its Myth and that of the Egyptian, Phoecenician, Samothracian, and Grecian Mysteries.

Plutarch teaches us what that object was. Like that of Masonry, it was Holiness, and purity of life and conversation, and the attainment of religious and philosophical Truth. So, too, he teaches us that the *Hieros Logos*, the Holy or Sacred Word or Doctrine was the true knowledge of the Nature of the Deity, hidden in myths and parables and symbols, and that of the immortality of the Soul. The Myth was, in substance (for the name of the Hero of the legend, and the details of the allegory varied in different countries, and are all unimportant and not of the essence of the Myth), the temporary death of the Personification of the Principle of Good and of Generation, slain by the Evil Principle, and rising again after a brief sojourn in the realms of darkness, to a new life. This was dramatically represented in the Mysteries; and in all of them the Candidate was made to represent the murdered Hero, and so was symbolically *born again.* In Egypt it was *Typhon* or *Set,* who slew *Osiris;* in Syrian *Atys* was slain, and in Phoenicia, *Tammuz* or *Adonis.*

Those from whom our ceremonial comes replaced these by *Hiram, Hurūm, or Khurūm,* a Phoenician artisan who worked upon the Temple built by the legendary Hebrew King שלמה , *Salamah* or *Shelomeh* [Peace, Prosperity, Reward, Perfection]. As usual, the name of the Hero is used to *conceal* and *hide* from the vulgar, but reveal to the Initiate the meaning and doctrine of initiation.

The name of the Artisan, or as we are in the habit of styling him, Architect, is given differently in different places in the Hebrew books, thus:

In 2 Chronicles 2:12, we have חורם אבי, *Khurm Abi.*

In 2 Samuel 5:11, and 5 Kings 5:16, חירם, *Khirm.*

In 2 Chronicles 4:11, חורם and חירם, *Khurm* and *Khirm.*

In 1 Kings 7:40, חירום, *Khirom* or *Khirum.*

In 2 Chronicles 4:16, חורם אביו, *Khurm Abiu, Abiv,* or *Abif.*

Gesenius renders, חורם , *Khurm, Khorm, Khiram, Huram,* or *Hūrūm,* by *Nobilis,*

Ingenuus; from חר.

Selig Newman renders חר, [בן חרים, Ben Khorim] a *Freemason,* a *Nobleman;* supposed to be called from the white robes they used to wear.

חור, *Khur,* means *white, noble,* an *aperature* through which the white light appears, *the opening of a window,* a *cavern,* the *socket of the eye.* חר, *Khi,* the root, means *free, freeborn;* חרי, *Khri,* also means *white,* and an *opening,* or the people who dwell in caves. חרם and חרש, *Khrs* or *Khris,* means the Sun—Job 9:7, and Judges 8:13; the *Orb* of the Sun, properly— Judges 14:8; Isaiah 19:18. חרש, *Khris,* also means an artificer, generally a smith, or worker in iron.

חרם, *Khrm,* means consecrated or devoted—either to God or to destruction.

The Persic word KHUR is the literal name of the *Sun.* From *Khur,* the Sun, comes *Chora,* a name of lower Egypt. Bryant says (*Mythology,* 1:48), "The Sun was likewise named Kur, Κύρος. Κύρον γάρ καλειν Πέρσας τὸν Ἡλιόν: Plutarch in *Artaxerxe,* 1012. Many places were sacred to this Deity, and called *Kura, Kuria, Kuropolis, Kurēnē, Kureschata, Kuresta, Kurestika Regio.*"[336]

In the Veda, the Sun is Sura and Surya, Hari and Harit; in Zend Hvare Khshaeta, in modern Persian Khorshid.

In Egypt we find this Trinity; Amun-Ra, the Creator, Osiris-Ra the Giver of Fruits, and Hor-us-Ra, the Giver of Light; the Summer, Autumn, and Spring Sun. [So *The Children of the Widow* (Isis), (so called because each in initiation had represented her Son, Hor-us), Devotees of *Huram, Khurom, Hor-Ra,* are ever advancing and journeying in search of *Light;* and the Sun appears on the ceilings of all their Temples, and is one of their three great Lights.]

Uhlemann says, "On account of the different effects of the Sun in the three Egyptian seasons of the year" [they had three only, instead of four, *the three gates of the Temple*], "this Deity appears in three forms, as Amun-Ra, Osiris-Ra, and Horus-Ra." (*Handbuch,* part 2, p. 168)

---

[336] Pike owned the 1807 reprint of Bryant's work (first ed. 1774), and slightly modified the text to emphasize the sound of letter *K*. The text actually reads, "The Sun was likewise named Kur, Cur, Κυρος. Κυρον γαρ καλειν Περσας τον Ἡλιον. Many places were sacred to this Deity, and called *Cura, Curia, Curopolis, Curene, Cureschata, Curesta, Curestica regio.*" —Jacob Bryant, *A New System; or, an Analysis of Ancient Mythology* 6 vols. (London, [England:] J. Walker, 1807), 1:48

In a papyrus published by Champollion, Aroenis, the Younger Horus, is styled "HAROERI, *Lord of the Solar Spirits, the beneficent Eye of the Sun:*" in which sense he bears some analogy to Apollo, who according to Plato, received his name from the emission of the rays of Light. Hor-Apollo says, "The Egyptians put *Lions* under the throne of *Horus*, this being their name for the Sun."

Other meanings connect themselves with this of the Sun, and illustrate and yet conceal the meaning of the ancient legend. Thus, analyzing the name חיראם, *Khiram,* we have חי, *Khi, living; Life.* (Leviticus 25:36) ראם, *Ram, was,* or prophetically, *shall be, raised, elevated, lifted up.* רום, *Rom, was raised, elevated, lifted up, raised himself.* (Lee, *Heb. Dict.*; *Selig Newman, Dict.; Genesis* 7:17; *Psalm* 46:10 or 11)

Thus חי יהוה , Khi Ihoh, as Ihoh liveth; חי אל , Khi Al, as Al liveth.

And ראם, *Ram,* the same as הרם, ארם, רום, *Rom, Aram,* and *Hrm, was lofty*; whence *Aram,* for Syria, or *Aramaa,* as *Highland.*

So that *Khiram* may be taken to mean, "Was raised up, living, or to life."

In Arabic, Hirm was an *Ox,* the symbol in Egypt of Osiris, or of the Sun in Taurus, at the Vernal Equinox.

חירה, Khirah, meant "nobility, a noble family."

According to *Menander,* Hiram first celebrated the resurrection of *Hercules* in the month Peritius (Berith); [*Movers,* 385; Josephus, *Antiq.,* 7:5, 3]; and *Movers* says [386], that on the 2d of Peritius, *the 25th of December* in the Roman calendar, the festival *Natalis Solis Invicti,* corresponding to the *Hercules Tyrius Invictus,* was celebrated; *and that* Hiram of Tyre *first performed this ceremony.*

אבי, Abi, not only means *father,* but *Progenitor; Abi yosheb ahel, the first* that made use of tents —Genesis 4:20; *Abi kal tepesh kanor, the first* of all such as handled the harp —Genesis 4:21.

The letter ו, *vav,* affixed to אבי and so making אביו, Abiv or Abiu, means "His," and the word thus compounded, "His Father"; in 2 Chronicles 4:16.

Plutarch says [*De Is. et Os.,* § 35]: "The Thyades, or Priestesses of Bacchus with their hymns endeavor to raise their God, whom they at that time distinguished by the name of *Winnower, Λικνίτης*"; in Hebrew רחת, *rukhet* (from the root רוח, *rukh,* (or, reversed, *khur,*) *Breath, Spirit*), *vannus, a winnowing fan*; in which, so reversed, the name of the Sun appears again.

Besides the general identity of the legend, there are not wanting in Plutarch coincidences between the Ancient and the Modern Rituals, even in the details.

"When the Egyptians sacrifice to the *Sun*, they strictly enjoin all those who approach to worship the God, *neither to wear any gold about them*, nor, etc."—*De Is. et Os.*, § 30.

"The seal of the Sphragista, an order of Priests peculiarly set apart.... Their impress, according to Castor, is *'a man upon his knees, with his hands tied behind him, and a sword pointed at his throat.'*"—*De Is. et Os.*, § 31.

When the ark or chest containing the body of Osiris had been carried by the waves of the sea to the coast of Byblos, [a city of the Phoenicians, between Tripoli and Berytus, not far from the sea, on a lofty site, called in Hebrew, גבל , *Gebal*, the residence of our *Giblemites*, in Greek *Byblos* or *Biblos*] it there gently lodged in the branches of a bush of *Tamarisk* [Erica], which in a short time had shot up into a large and beautiful tree, growing round the chest and enclosing it on every side. The King of Byblos, astonished at its unusual size, had it cut down, and made that part of the trunk in which the chest was enclosed, a pillar to support the roof of his house—[*Is. et Os.*, § 15]. The real sepulcher of Osiris is also said to be in the little island which the Nile makes at Phila where his tomb "is overshadowed with the branches of *a tamarisk tree, whose bigness exceeds that of an olive.*" —Ibid., § 21.

In the sacred dirge or lamentation which the Priests made over Osiris, they "bewailed him who was born on the *right* side of the world, and who perished on the *left*." Perhaps the alternation of right and left in the first two degrees of Masonry, has a concealed allusion to this; and there is perhaps, in "the rough sands of the sea," an allusion to the fact, that the Egyptian Priests "expressed an abhorrence, both toward the *Sea*, as well as *Salt*; calling this latter *Typhon's foam*, and amongst their other prohibitions, forbidding it to be ever laid upon their tables."—*De Is. et Os.*, § 32.

Perhaps there is no symbol in Masonry for whose presence among our emblems it has been found so difficult to account, and which has been so persistently let alone, as the 47th Problem of Euclid, which figures in all our Monitors, as much out of place as an Etruscan cornice-stone in a Roman hovel. We know its meaning now, but Plutarch did not, nor did Iamblichus. It had been lost long before they lived. Pythagoras had too carefully concealed it; and these later writers looked in the wrong direction for it. Plutarch's explanation, altogether wrong, is as follows.

"Now universal Nature, in its utmost and most perfect extent, may be considered as made up of these three things, of *Intelligence* of *Matter* and of that which is the result of both these, in the Greek language called *Kosmos*, a word which equally signifies, either *Beauty* and *Order*, or the *World* itself. The first of these is the same with what Plato is wont to call the Idea, the *Exemplar* and the *Father* to the second of them he has given the name of the *Mother*, the *Nurse* and the *place and receptacle of generation*; and to the latter of them that of the *offspring* and the *production*."

———

"So again, with regard to the Egyptians, there is good reason to conclude, that they were wont to liken the Universal Nature to what they called the most beautiful and perfect Triangle; the same as does Plato himself, in that nuptial diagram, as it is termed, which he has introduced into his Commonwealth. Now in this Triangle, which is rectangular, the perpendicular side is imagined equal to *three*, the base to *four*, and the hypotenuse which is equal [whose *square* is equal] to the [*squares* of the] other two containing sides, to *five*. [$3 \times 3 = 9$, $4 \times 4 = 16$, $5 \times 5 = 25$, $9 + 16 = 25$; which is the 47th Proposition of Euclid.] In this scheme, therefore, we must suppose, that the *perpendicular* is designed by them to represent, the masculine Nature, the base the feminine, and that the hypotenuse is to be looked upon as the offspring of both; and accordingly the first of them will aptly enough represent *Osiris* or the Prime Cause; the second, *Isis*, or the receptive Power; the last *Horus* or the common effect of the other two. For 3 is the first number which is composed of both even and odd; and 4 is a square whose side is equal to the first even number 2; but 5, being generated as it were, out of both the preceding numbers, 2 and 3 be said to have an equal relation to both of them as to its common parents." —Ibid. § 56.

Plutarch considers Isis to be "the feminine part of Nature, or that property of Nature which renders herself a fit subject for the production of all other beings; for which reason it is that Plato calls her, the *Nurse*, a All-Receiver, and that she is vulgarly termed *Myrionymus*, or the myriad-named Goddess; noting hereby that capacity, with which she is endued, of receiving and being converted into all manner of forms and species, which it shall please the Supreme Reason to impress upon her." —*De Is. et Os.*, § 53.

The Temple of Solomon, like every Lodge, is a Symbol of Isis or Universal Nature; and the works of the Supreme Reason are symbolized by the labors of Hiram upon the Temple, and the columns, vessels, and fabrics that he produced.

"The Soul of Osiris," we are told, "is, eternal and incorruptible, though his body is often torn to pieces and hidden by Typhon, and as often searched after, found again, and joined together by the wandering Isis. For that Being *of whose essence it is to exist*" [יהוה], "to be Intelligent and to be Good, is so far from being corruptible, that He is not obnoxious to the least degree of mutability; though, at the same time, those images, those delineations, forms and likenesses, which the material and passive part of Nature hath taken off as it were, from him, and received upon herself, those, it must be owned, like the impressions of a seal upon wax are not permanent and everlasting, but liable to the attacks of that unruly and turbulent Power, who was driven hither from above, and who makes constant war upon Horus, or that visible image of the Intellectual world which was born of Isis." —*De Is. et Os.* § 4.

"They further add," says Plutarch, "that Isis and Osiris, having a mutual affection enjoyed each other in their mother's womb before they were born; and that from this commerce sprang *Aroeris*, the Egyptians likewise call the Elder *Horus*, and the Greeks Apollo." —*De Is. et Os.*, § 12. As in the Kabbalah, in כתר, Keter [the first Sephirah, the *Will* of Deity, yet *unexpressed*, yet unmanifested outwardly], are as in a *matrix*, Hokmah and Binah the Divine Wisdom in the Deity, and the same acting as the Human Understanding, the second and third Sephiroth; and therein; while they are as yet un-emanated, the former begets and the latter produces, Da'at, or Intellection, the *Thinking* of men, yet unuttered in Thought; and wherein are included, again as in a matrix and unevolved, Gevurah and Gedulah, or Chesed, *Justice* and *Mercy*, which, therein uniting, as it were sexually, produce *Beauty* or *Harmony*, Tiferet, the sixth Sephirah. In this again are included, and out of it flow forth Netzach, or *Success, Victory*, and Hod, *Glory*, the seventh and eighth Sephiroth; from which proceeds *Stability* or Permanency, Immutability in the designs of Deity, the ninth Sephirah; and from that results Imperial Dominion and Supreme Control, Malakoth, the tenth Sephirah, of the Deity, over all that is, Evil as well as Good.

Among the Egyptians, the Sun was particularly consecrated to Osiris, and the Lion was worshipped by them, and the doors of their temples ornamented with the gaping jaws of this animal; because the Nile first began to flow whilst the Sun was in the constellation Leo. — [*De Is. et Os.,* § 38.] We may, perhaps, find in this a hint to serve as a key to the meaning of "the strong grip of the Lion's paw."

It is said that when Pythagoras discovered the 47th Theorem of Euclid, he sacrificed a *hecatomb* for joy. A ἑκατόμβη was strictly an offering of a hundred oxen; but even in Homer it had lost its etymological signification and signified only a great public sacrifice. We find in the *Iliad* mention made of a hecatomb of *twelve* oxen, and of hecatombs of sheep.

This theorem is, that in every right-angled triangle, the sum of the squares of the lengths of the base and perpendicular is equal to the square of the length of the hypotenuse.

As a mere mathematical theorem or proposition, this is of no especial importance, and has no special significance. Its principal *practical* use is, that if one erects a perpendicular line upon a base line, making one three measures and the other four, he will have one at an exact right angle with the other, if he connects the ends by a line of five measures. As a theorem it has no philosophical or religious value. To give it such a value, it must be in some manner a symbol. Pythagoras could not have so greatly exulted at discovering, if he did discover, this mere mathematical theorem, how ever valuable the knowledge of such theorems then may have been. There were fifty others equally as valuable.

He must have discovered in it and in the figure and numbers representing it, a new symbol, unknown or unnoticed before, of some ancient and valuable, truth or doctrine. To be able to add another symbol to those already known and used by the Sages who possessed the truth or doctrine, was worth a public sacrifice.

Plutarch, supposing that Pythagoras brought his doctrine and its symbols from Egypt, wrote the whole treatise *Peri Isidos kai Osiridos* on that theory. He says that the base, of 3 measures, meant Isis, and the perpendicular, of 4, Osiris.

But why these numbers should represent them, it was not in his power to explain, otherwise than by saying that the hypotenuse represented Horus, their issue, and if it measures 5, the other sides must measure 3 and 4.

Why should Horus, the issue, measure 5, excelling by so much his father, Osiris? Certainly, he gives no reason for this, and there could be none. The *religious* explanation, according to Plutarch's interpretation, would be, Horus is equal to the squares of Osiris and Isis, added together. According to his explanation, the symbol taught no doctrine whatever, and was not in any sense mysterious.

Other and much more apt symbols would represent Father, Mother, and Child or Issue.

Plutarch, like Iamblichus, was utterly ignorant of the meaning of what Pythagoras taught as to numbers. None of the scholars now know what he meant and they never will, while they look to Egypt or to books written long after his death for the explanation. He did *not* mean that the Deity created by the instrumentality of, abstract numbers.

But this figure *was* connected with his theories as to numbers, and in fact, its whole meaning consists in the numbers 3, 4, and 5, which the side of the triangle represent and measure.

The Masters of the Royal Secret know what the symbol and its numbers did mean, to Pythagoras, and do not wonder that he was overjoyed to add it to the existing symbols, which, to those whom he taught to read them, expressed the Holy Doctrine. Sancta Sanctis.

No doubt the *doctrine* taught in the Mysteries, was that of Pythagoras, and that of which the legends of Osiris and Isis, Adonis and the Boar, Hiram, and his assassins were the symbols. "It is impossible," Plutarch thinks, "that any one cause, whatever, be it bad or even good (for God cannot be the author of any evil), should be the common Principle of all things!"

"For," he says, "the harmony of the world, like that of a harp (to use the expression of Heraclites), is made up of discords, and consists in a mixture of good and evil; or, as Euripides has it, 'Good and Evil cannot be separate from each other,' though they are so tempered as that beauty and order are the result. From hence, therefore, arose that very ancient opinion which has been handed down from the Theologists and Legislators to the Poets and Philosophers; an opinion which, though its first author is unknown, has nevertheless gained so firm and established a credit every where, as not only to be commonly talked of by both Greeks and Barbarians, *but to be even taught by them in their mysteries and in their sacrifices*: namely, that the world is neither wholly left to its own motions, without some Mind, some Superior Reason to guide and govern it; nor that it is *one* such Mind only or Reason, that, as it were with a helm or bridle, steers and directs the whole; but, as there are many things wherein the Good and Evil are equally blended together, or, rather indeed, as nature produces nothing here below without such mixture, and as it cannot be supposed that one and the same Being is the dispenser of these contrarieties, distributing, as it were from two different vessels the several distinct portions of Good and Evil—for this reason, I say, was first introduced the opinion, that this mixture which is observed in human life, this inequality and variety which are discerned in the universe, and all those changes which we see in it, at least in these sublunary regions, are owing to two contrary Principles, to two quite different and distinct Powers.... For, if nothing can come into being without cause, and if that which is perfectly Good cannot be the cause of Evil then must there needs be a distinct Principle in Nature, as well for the production of Evil as of that is Good." —*De Is. et Os.*, § 45.

Plutarch proceeds to say that some philosophers term these two Principles two Gods; while others call the Good one, only, God, and the evil one Demon; like *Ζωρόαστρις ὁ Μάγος*, the Magos Zoroastris, "who is reported to have lived five thousand years before the Trojan War." "He called the Good Principle *Ὡρομάζη* (Hōrŏmazē), and the Evil One *Ἀρειμάνιος* (Areimanios), adding, moreover, that as of all sensible Beings, the former bore the greatest resemblance to Light, so the latter was most like *darkness.*" —*De Is. et Os.*, § 46.

The Magian Philosophers, he says, tell us, "that Ormuzd sprang originally from the purest Light, and Ahriman from the most profound darkness. The former created six Gods, and the latter created six, of different natures and operations, to oppose them. Then the former adorned the Heaven with Stars, placing the Sun in front of all the rest; and then each created twenty-four other Gods, which intermingling, Evil and Good became blended. For four terms of 3,000 years each, these Gods are to contend with varied success, each alternately victorious and depressed; at the end of which time Ahriman is to be destroyed, and mankind for the future to live in perfect happiness." —*De Is. et Os.*, § 47.

The doctrine of the Magi, in his day, was what it is now, a total misapprehension of the original Irano-Aryan creed. Anra-Mainyus, the Malign Mind, was not the antagonist of Ahura Mazda, who had no rival, but was the Creator, Supreme over all. This Evil Mind was the negative, and so the opponent, not of the Supreme Deity Himself, the Divine Light and Splendor, but of the Divine Wisdom immanent in him, Cpĕnta-Mainyu, the Beneficent Mind or Intellect. Ahura Mazda was not the offspring of Zĕrvana Akarana, the Infinite Time, but was said to have created *in* the Infinite Time the words spoken by him.

The Chaldæans also had beneficent and evil Planetary Gods; the Greeks had two Jupiters the Olympian and Pluto, and made *Harmonia* to be the offspring of Mars and Venus. Heraclitus said that *Discord* would never exceed the proper bounds allotted to it; for should this ever happen to be the case, *the Fates, avengers of what is right, would find it out.* The Pythagoreans had a great number of terms, which they made use of to express the contrary natures of these two Principles; calling the Good One, "The Unit, the Definite, the Fixed, the Straight, the Odd, the Square, the Equal, the Right, and the Light or Lucid"; and the Evil One, "the Duad, the Indefinite, the Mobile, the Crooked, the Even, the Oblong, the Unequal, the Left [Sinister] and the Dark." Anaxagoras calls the one *Intelligence*, and the other *Infinity*. (*De Is[ide] et Os[iride]*, § 48)

> By Osiris we are to understand those faculties of the Universal Soul, such as Intelligence and Reason, which are, as it were, the Supreme Lords and Directors of all that is Good.... On the contrary, those Powers of the Universal Soul, which are subject to the influence of passions, the boisterous, the irrational and the unruly part of it, may be called Typhon. (ibid., § 49)

> When the Supreme Reason composed this Universe, He made one harmonious system, even out of the most discordant principles, and did not utterly destroy, though He greatly maimed the Power of the Evil Being. (ibid. § 55)

We thus see, and by many other passages, that notwithstanding what Plutarch says elsewhere in regard to the two Principles, he had learned the True Doctrine in regard to the real nature of the Deity, and believed in the ONE, Single, Simple, Supreme GOD; and that, in what he said as to the Two Principles, he meant to hint at the great doctrine, taught in the Mysteries, that Evil is a *necessary* concomitant of Good; that discords as well as concords concur to produce harmony; that Evil is the occasion and *cause* of Good; that contraries sympathize, and opposites harmonize; that the universe is a system of *equilibria*, in which Truth is only evolved by collision and discussion; and the seemingly *in*consistent are the most consistent of all things. What more inconsistent, to our minds, than infinite Justice and *infinite* mercy? They seem two parallel lines, that will never even approach each other; if not two, infinitely diverging. But Geburah and Gedulah meet in The Infinite, and harmonize, *and are essentially one*; and from them flow forth Perfect Harmony in all the Universe, the Success and Glory of God, the Stability of His plans, and the absolute undivided Empire which Evil does *not* share with Him, over the Universe.

> Upon the whole, however, Osiris, or the Good Principle, has the superiority. (*De Is[ide] et Os[iride]*, § 59)

> Osiris likewise is a compounded name, being derived from *Osion* and *Hieron*; for, as he is supposed to be that common Reason which pervades both the Superior and Life nor regions of the Ur by the latter of these terms the ancients would denote him in his, celestial capacity, as by the former of them they would express his terrestrial and infernal influence. (ibid., § 61)

He significantly tells us that "those who have not learned to make use of *words* in their true sense, will be apt to mistake, likewise, in things themselves." (ibid., § 71)

The Divine Reason," he tells us, "stands not in speech; but marching through still and silent paths Administers the world with Justice." (|ibid., § 75|)[337]

> The Mind and Reason of the Supreme God, which in its own nature is invisible to us, and dwelling in obscurity, by putting itself in motion proceeds to the production of other beings.... That one Supreme Reason, who framed this world, and that one Providence that governs and watches over the whole.... That God who orders and directs all things.... Whatever Beings are endowed with life, with the faculty of seeing, that have in them a principle of voluntary motion, and that are able to distinguish What belongs to and what is proper for them, and what not, all these are to be regarded as the outflowings" [effluxes], "as it were, or as so many portions taken off from that Supreme Providential

---

[337] Although not noticed by Pike, Plutarch's original Greek text is a quote from Hecuba's declaration to Zeus in Euripedes, *Toades*, 887–888.

Wisdom, that governs the Universe.... As Osiris is a First Principle, prior to all other Beings, and purely intelligent, he must ever remain unmixed and undefiled ... that First simple and immaterial Being, *whom truly to know, and to be able to approach with purity,* is, according to both Plato and Aristotle, the highest pitch of Perfection which Philosophy can arrive at." (*De Is[ide] et Os[iride]*, § 62, 67, 77, 78)

And Plutarch thus hints at the Work of the Initiates, and at the results and benefits of the *palingenesis* the *being born again*, of initiation: "The souls and minds of men are looked upon as the matter" [the *Materia*, the rough Ashlar or marble in the quarry or block], "of Knowledge and Virtue; and as such are delivered up to *Reason* to be polished and modeled by it into their due form and shape; thus some philosophers have even called the Mind the place of our ideas, and the workshop" [the usual and favorite name, *atelier*, of our French Brethren, for their Lodges], "as it were, wherein all our notions are engraved [or impressed], and formed." (*De Is[ide] et Os[iride]*, § 58)

> There is nothing by which a man approaches nearer the Divinity than by right *Reason*, especially when it is employed in religious matters; nor anything which is of greater moment to his happiness; wherefore it is, that every one *who intends to consult the oracle,* is strictly charged upon the spot, that he "take care 'to have pious thoughts in his heart, 'and seemly and decent words in his mouth." (ibid., § 68)

> As, therefore, the souls of men are not able to participate of that Divine Nature, whilst they are thus encompassed about with bodies and passions, any further than by those obscure glimmerings, which they may be able to attain unto, as it were in a confused dream, through means of philosophy—so, when they are freed from these impediments, and remove into those *purer* and *unseen* regions, which are neither discernible by our present senses nor liable to accidents of any kind, it is then that this God Osiris becomes their Leader and their King; upon him they wholly depend, still beholding

without satiety, and still ardently longing after that Beauty, which it is not possible for man to express or conceive." (ibid., § 79)

It is but a little while since the first attempt was made to discover the true meaning of the ceremonies and symbols of Blue Masonry. No one had, until then, looked in the right direction for these meanings. The symbols were sphinxes, whose real meaning no one knew. Perhaps we have not yet learned the meaning of all. The field of study is wide and large, and there are few to work in it.

We know now the real meaning of the compasses and square upon the altar: the two points under the square at initiation, then one, then both, above it.[338]

We know the true meaning of the three grips, by the last of which the body was raised.[339]

We know meaning of the three blows inflicted on Hiram at the three gates, and of the implements used.[340]

We know the whole meaning of the Mystic Numbers, the Holy Doctrine, and the Royal Secret.[341]

We know the meaning of the Eagle, Intellect; of the Man, Thought; of the Ox, Strength; of the Lion, Sovereignty, on the Standards of the four principal tribes of Israel.

But much remains to be discovered yet, and will in time become known. Take the two columns at the Porch of the Temple! Hear these sentences, which we borrow for the occasion, and decide whether they refer to those columns—the *Active* Force or Energy and the *Passive* Stability or Permanence?

"The first Sages who sought for the cause of causes, saw Good and Evil in the world; they observed the Shadow, and the Light; they compared Winter with Spring, Old Age with Youth, Life with Death, and said: 'The First Cause is Beneficent and Cruel; It *gives life* and *destroys*.'

"Are there then *two* contrary Principles, a Good and an Evil?" cries the disciples of Manes.

"No! The two Principles of the Universal Equilibrium are *not* contrary to each other, though in apparent opposition; for it is a Single Wisdom that opposes the one to the other."

---

338 "Lesson 1, The Compasses and Square," Pike, *Esoterika* (2005), 91–106
339 "Lesson III, The Three Grips," Pike, *Esoterika* (2005), 125–37
340 "Lesson 2, The Weapons and Blows of the Assassins," Pike, *Esoterika* (2005), 107–23
341 The explanations of these are provided in the rituals.

"The Good is on the *right*; the Evil on the *left*; but THE SUPREME GOOD *is above both*, and makes the Evil subserve the triumph of the Good, and the Good serve for the reparation of the Evil."

Surely the subject of Masonic Symbolism is not yet exhausted. God, Pythagoras said, is the living and absolute Truth clothed in Light: the Word is Number manifested by Form:

God is the supreme Music, of which Nature is the Harmony. There is, he said, a triple Word, for the hierarchical order always manifests itself by three. There are the word simple, the word hieroglyphical, and the word symbolic; in other terms, the word that expresses, the word that conceals, and the word that signifies: all hieratic intelligence is in the perfect knowledge of these three degrees.

Let the Student of Masonic Symbolism ponder on these sayings.

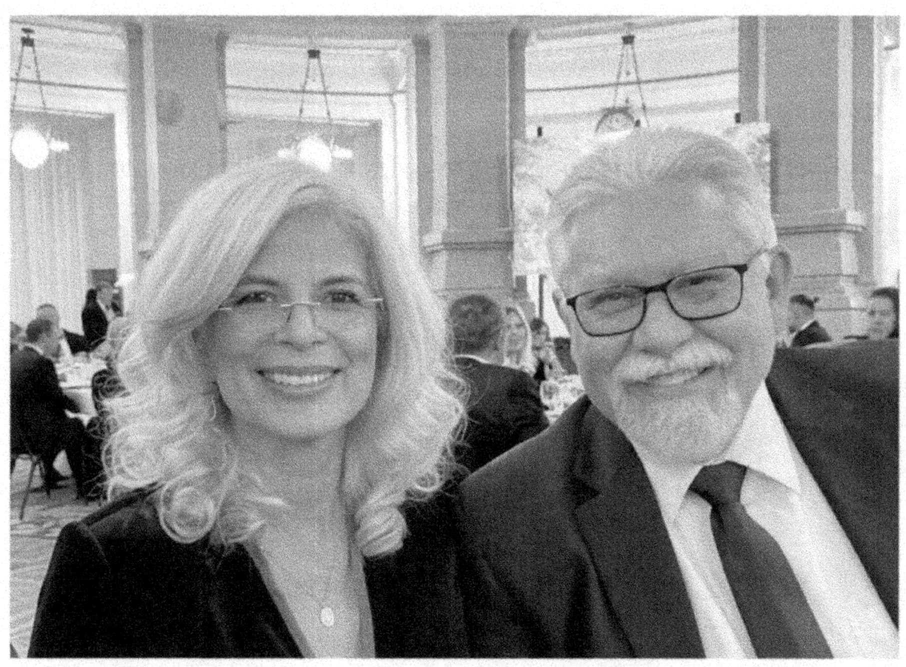

Arturo de Hoyos, 33°, Grand Cross, KYCH,
is Grand Archivist and Grand Historian of the Supreme Council, 33°,
Southern Jurisdiction,
Washington, DC, and a member of the executive staff at the House of
the Temple.

HIS PREVIOUS BOOKS INCLUDE:

The Cloud of Prejudice: A Study in Anti-Masonry (1992)

Rituals of the Masonic Grand Lodge of the Sun, Bayreuth, Germany (1992)

Liturgy of Germania Lodge No. 46 F&AM (1993)

The Book of the Words—Sephir H'Debarim: With an Introduction by Art de Hoyos (1999)
[Serbian edition, 2017]

Albert Pike's Esoterika: The Symbolism of the Blue Degrees of Freemasonry (2005)
[Serbian ed., 2015; Spanish ed., 2016; Bulgarian ed., 2021]

The Scottish Rite Ritual Monitor and Guide (2007)

Light on Masonry: The History and Rituals of America's Most Important Masonic Expose (2008)

Masonic Formulas and Rituals Transcribed by Albert Pike (2010)

Albert Pike's Morals and Dogma: Annotated Edition (2011)
[Bulgarian edition, 2022]

Freemasonry's Royal Secret (2014)
[Serbian ed., 2017]

Reprints of Rituals of Old Degrees (2015)

A Lecture on the Masonic Tracing Boards (2017)
[Bulgaria ed., 2017]

Albert Pike's Magnum Opus (2017)
[Bulgarian ed., 2019]

Curiosities and Treasures (2019)

The Freemason's Punchbowl (2020)

Insignia of Office and Honor (2021)

A House Adorned for Beauty (2022)

Supreme Council Souvenir Medallions, 1969–2021 (2023)

Albert Pike's The Porch and the Middle Chamber, The Book of the Lodge (2023)
[Bulgarian ed., 2019]

IN COLLABORATION WITH S. BRENT MORRIS:

Is It True What They Say About Freemasonry? The Methods of Anti-Masons (1994)

Freemasonry in Context: History, Ritual, Controversy (2004)

Committed to the Flames: The History and Rituals of a Secret Masonic Rite (2008)

The Most Secret Mysteries of the High Degrees of Masonry Unveiled (2011)
[Serbian ed., 2017]

Allegorical Conversations Arranged by Wisdom (2012)

Cerneauism and American Freemasonry (2019)

The Perfect Ceremonies of Craft Masonry and the Holy Royal Arch (2021)

Samuel Prichard's Masonry Dissected (2022)

Three Distinct Knocks & Jachin and Boaz (2026)

IN COLLABORATION WITH JOSEF WÄGES:

Étienne Morin: From the French Rite to the Scottish Rite (2024) [Romanian ed., 2025]

Julius F. Saches's Ancient Documents Relating to the A. & A. Scottish Rite (2024)

IN COLLABORATION WITH B. CHRIS RULI:

(ed./intro) *William Boyden's Chronology of the Supreme Council 1801–1859* (2024)

Lodges of Sorrow: Craft, Rose Croix, Kadosh (2025)

Ray Baker Harris's "Eleven Gentlemen of Charleston," 125th Anniversary Edition (2026)

AS EDITOR AND/OR AUTHOR OF INTRODUCTION/PREFACE/FOREWORD:

(ed.) *Collectanea* (Grand College of Rites, 1994–2025)

(ed.) *Miscellanea* (Grand Council, Allied Masonic Degrees, 2001–02)

(ed.) C.F. Kleinknecht, *Forms and Traditions of the Scottish Rite* (2001)

(ed.) L.P. Watkins, *Albert Pike's String of Pearls* (2008)

(ed.) L.P. Watkins, *International Masonic Collection, 1723–2011* (2012)

(intro.) S. Dafoe, Morgan: *The Scandal the Shook Freemasonry* (2009)

(intro.) A. Bernheim, *Un certaine idee de la franc-maconnerie* (2009)

(ed./intro.) R. L. Hutchens, *A Bridge to Light: A Study in Masonic Ritual & Philosophy* (2010)

(preface) A. de Keghel, *Le defi Maconnique Americain* (2015)

(preface) A. de Keghel, *American Freemasonry* (2017)

(preface) D. L. Harrison, *The Lost Rites of Freemasonry* (2017)

(foreword) Mark Stavish, *The Path of Freemasonry: The Craft as a Spiritual Practice* (2021)

(forword) Billy J. Hamilton, *A Stranger in the Elemental Temple* (2024)

Related Titles from Westphalia Press

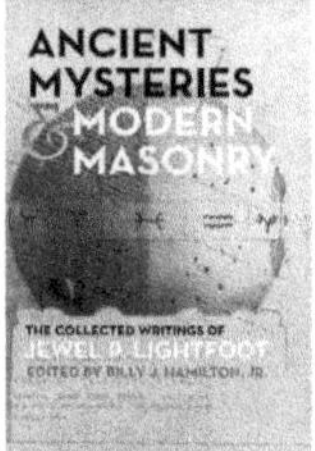

Ancient Mysteries and Modern Masonry: The Collected Writings of Jewel P. Lightfoot, Edited by Billy J. Hamilton Jr.

Jewel P. Lightfoot. Former Attorney General of the State of Texas. Past Grand Master of the Masonic Grand Lodge of Texas. From humble beginnings in rural Arkansas, he worked to become an educated man who excelled in law and Freemasonry. He was a gentleman of his time, well-known as a scholar, public speaker, and Masonic philosopher.

Essay on The Mysteries and the True Object of The Brotherhood of Freemasons
by Jason Williams

This isn't a reprint of a classic. It's a new rendition with new life breathed into it, to be enjoyed both by the layperson trying to understand the Craft and Masonic scholars taking a deeper dive into the fraternity's golden years—when the concepts of liberty and equality were still fresh.

Female Emancipation and Masonic Membership:
An Essential Collection
By Guillermo De Los Reyes Heredia

Female Emancipation and Masonic Membership: An Essential Combination is a collection of essays on Freemasonry and gender that promotes a transatlantic discussion of the study of the history of women and Freemasonry and their contribution in different countries.

Freemasonry, Heir to the Enlightenment
by Cécile Révauger

Modern Freemasonry may have mythical roots in Solomon's time but is really the heir to the Enlightenment. Ever since the early eighteenth century freemasons have endeavored to convey the values of the Enlightenment in the cultural, political and religious fields, in Europe, the American colonies and the emerging United States.

Masonic Myths and Legends
by Pierre Mollier

Freemasonry preserves the teachings of a primitive Judeo-Christian gnosis. In order to better understand these legends and myths and their significance, Pierre Mollier has studied their origins and attempted to find their sources.

Exploring the Vault: Masonic Higher Degrees 1730–1800
by John Belton and Roger Dachez

The study adopted a forensic approach to the available evidence, and the discoveries exceeded expectations. The book details their 'archaeological finds' and offers a novel perspective on the development of the Higher Degrees during the eighteenth century.

Étienne Morin: From the French Rite to the Scottish Rite by Arturo de Hoyos and Josef Wäges

All extant Masonic records have been consulted and using this meta-data, a comprehensive reconstruction emerges, revealing that Étienne Morin was a founding masonic figure in Saint Domingue and creator of his own high degree system, that operated for a time as a defacto Grand Lodge.

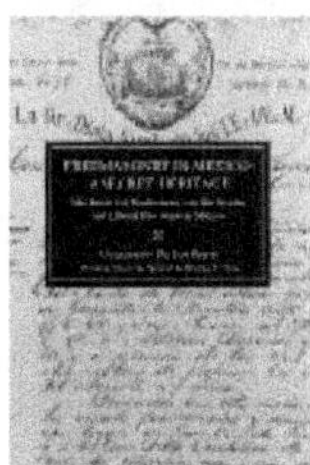

The Impact of Freemasonry on the Secular and Liberal Discourse in Mexico
by Guillermo De Los Reyes, Translated by Bradley L. Drew

In this thought-provoking book, De Los Reyes argues that Freemasonry, through its lodges, played a decisive role in shaping Mexico's national thought, contributing to the creation of a liberal and secular State and fostering anticlerical sentiments among the laity that endured well into the twentieth century.

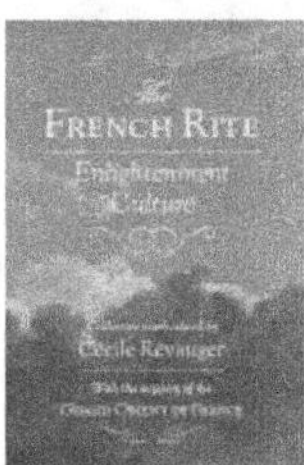

The French Rite: Enlightenment Culture
Cécile Révauger, Editor

This book, focused on the French Rite, covers the founding principles of the Enlightenment and their influence on the birth of modern Freemasonry as we know it today. The authors revisit the fundamental values of the Enlightenment, from a rational approach to religious tolerance and cosmopolitanism.

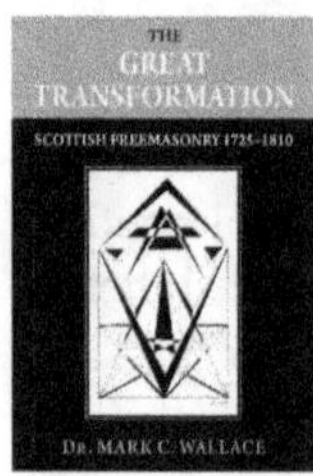

The Great Transformation: Scottish Freemasonry 1725-1810
by Dr. Mark C. Wallace

This book examines Scottish Freemasonry in its wider British and European contexts between the years 1725 and 1810. The Enlightenment effectively crafted the modern mason and propelled Freemasonry into a new era marked by growing membership and the creation of the Grand Lodge of Scotland.

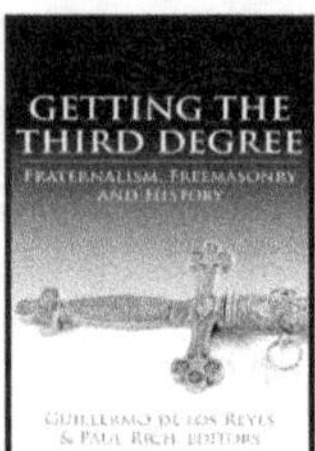

Getting the Third Degree: Fraternalism, Freemasonry and History
Edited by Guillermo De Los Reyes and Paul Rich

As this engaging collection demonstrates, the doors being opened on the subject range from art history to political science to anthropology, as well as gender studies, sociology and more. The organizations discussed may insist on secrecy, but the research into them belies that.

Freemasonry: A French View
by Roger Dachez and Alain Bauer

Perhaps one should speak not of Freemasonry but of Freemasonries in the plural. In each country Masonic historiography has developed uniqueness. Two of the best known French Masonic scholars present their own view of the worldwide evolution and challenging mysteries of the fraternity over the centuries.

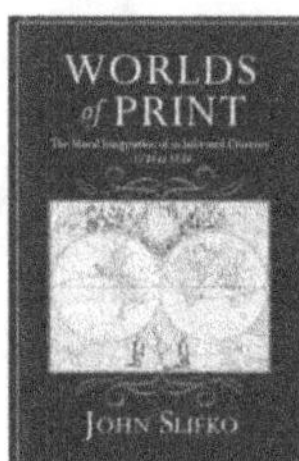

Worlds of Print: The Moral Imagination of an Informed Citizenry, 1734 to 1839
by John Slifko

John Slifko argues that freemasonry was representative and played an important role in a larger cultural transformation of literacy and helped articulate the moral imagination of an informed democratic citizenry via fast emerging worlds of print.

Why Thirty-Three?: Searching for Masonic Origins
by S. Brent Morris, PhD

What "high degrees" were in the United States before 1830? What were the activities of the Order of the Royal Secret, the precursor of the Scottish Rite? A complex organization with a lengthy pedigree like Freemasonry has many basic foundational questions waiting to be answered, and that's what this book does: answers questions.

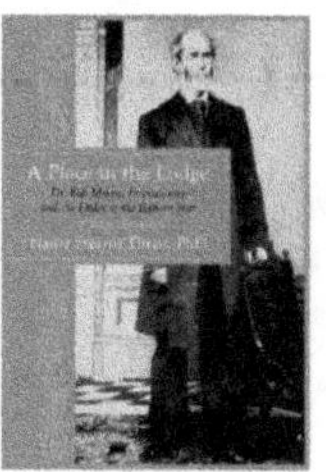

A Place in the Lodge: Dr. Rob Morris, Freemasonry and the Order of the Eastern Star
by Nancy Stearns Theiss, PhD

Ridiculed as "petticoat masonry," critics of the Order of the Eastern Star did not deter Rob Morris' goal to establish a Masonic organization that included women as members. Morris carried the ideals of Freemasonry through a despairing time of American history.

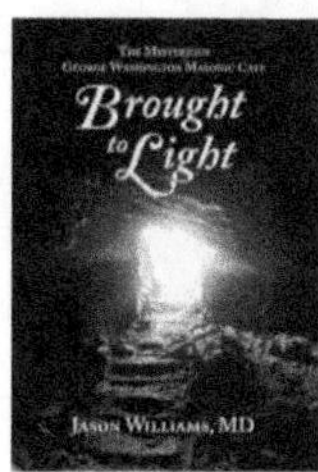

Brought to Light: The Mysterious George Washington Masonic Cave
by Jason Williams MD

The George Washington Masonic Cave near Charles Town, West Virginia, contains a signature carving of George Washington dated 1748. This book painstakingly pieces together the chronicled events and real estate archives related to the cavern in order to sort out fact from fiction.

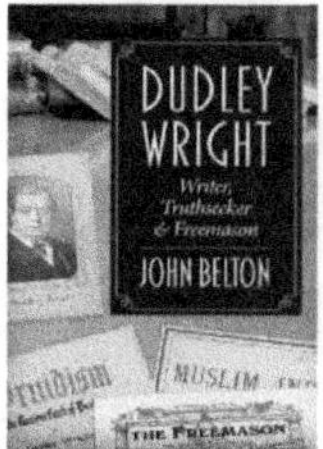

Dudley Wright: Writer, Truthseeker & Freemason
by John Belton

Dudley Wright (1868-1950) was an Englishman and professional journalist who took a universalist approach to the various great Truths of Life. He travelled though many religions in his life and wrote about them all, but was probably most at home with Islam.

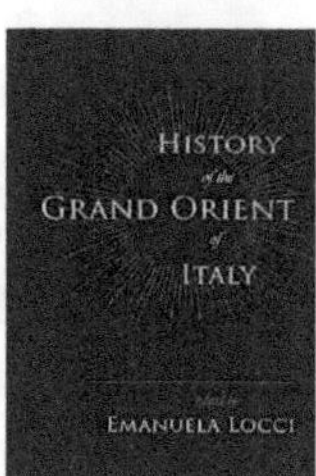

History of the Grand Orient of Italy
Emanuela Locci, Editor

No book in Masonic literature upon the history of Italian Freemasonry has been edited in English up to now. This work consists of eight studies, covering a span from the Eighteenth Century to the end of the WWII, tracing through the story, the events and pursuits related to the Grand Orient of Italy.

westphaliapress.org

www.ingramcontent.com/pod-product-compliance
Lightning Source LLC
Chambersburg PA
CBHW080327030726
47593CB00010B/2912